"Safe & Caring Schools provides educators with the roadmap and all the tools necessary to transform classrooms and schools into environments that are not only physically, socially, and emotionally safe, but that engage and nurture our children's resilience, including their capacity and love for learning."

BONNIE BENARD,
SENIOR PROGRAM ASSOCIATE, WESTED,
OAKLAND, CALIFORNIA

SAFE & CARING SCHOOLS ®

Activities for Building Character and Social-Emotional Learning

GRADES 1–2

Katia S. Petersen, Ph.D.

free spirit
PUBLISHING®

Activities for Building Character and Social-Emotional Learning Grades 1–2 was previously published as *Safe & Caring Schools Grades 1–2*.

Library of Congress Cataloging-in-Publication Data
Petersen, Katia.
   Activities for building character and social-emotional learning. Grades 1–2 / Katia S. Petersen.
      p. cm. — (Safe & caring schools)
   Originally published under the title: Safe & caring schools. Grades 1–2, c2008.
   Summary: "Hundreds of user-friendly lesson plans help teachers build attitudes of respect and caring, reduce problem behaviors, empower students to solve problems, and educate the whole child socially, emotionally, and academically. The lessons' literature-based connections allow teachers to 'build in' rather than 'add on' social-emotional learning (SEL) as part of the daily curriculum. Each resource guide offers: Monthly themes focused on emotions, empathy, relationships, conflict resolution, bullying prevention, problem solving, decision making, teamwork, and self-esteem; Literature-based lessons with curriculum integrations for using the lessons as part of language arts, social studies, science, math, art, and music; Easy-to-implement lesson formats for all activities: Read, Discuss, Do, Relate; Built-in assessments; Reproducible activity handouts in the book and on CD-ROM. Field-tested in classrooms across the United States, these activities when fully implemented have resulted in improved school climate, greater parent engagement, increased academic achievement, and reduction in discipline referrals. The Activities for Building Character and Social-Emotional Learning resource guides are essential teaching tools for all preK–8 teachers"—Provided by publisher.
   ISBN 978-1-57542-392-0
 1. Classroom management—United States. 2. School environment—United States. 3. Learning, Psychology of. 4. Moral education (Primary) 5. Affective education. 6. Education, Primary—Activity programs. I. Petersen, Katia. Safe & caring schools. Grades 1–2. II. Title.
   LB3013.P4334 2012
   372.1102'4—dc23
                                             2011053531

eBook ISBN: 978-1-57542-667-6

Edited by Deborah Verdoorn Anderson and Eric Braun
Visual identity design by Tilka Design
Design by Katrin Loss, Tilka Design, and activity page design by J Campbell, ArtVille
Illustrations by Brie Spangler

10 9 8 7 6 5 4 3 2 1
Printed in the United States of America

Free Spirit Publishing Inc.
Minneapolis, MN
(612) 338-2068
help4kids@freespirit.com
www.freespirit.com

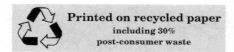
Printed on recycled paper
including 30%
post-consumer waste

As a member of the Green Press Initiative, Free Spirit Publishing is committed to the three Rs: Reduce, Reuse, Recycle. Whenever possible, we print our books on recycled paper containing a minimum of 30% post-consumer waste. At Free Spirit it's our goal to nurture not only children, but nature too!

green press INITIATIVE

Dedication

This book is dedicated to the thousands of children in my life who give me inspiration and inner strength to do my part in creating a safe and caring world. It is my hope that these resources help connect children, parents, and educators so they may achieve success wherever life takes them.

Acknowledgments

Safe & Caring Schools (SCS) has been tested where it matters most—in the classrooms. As such, my gratitude goes to all the teachers, specialists, and others who took time to incorporate the content of this guide into their lesson plans and then provide feedback about its efficacy. Efforts to create safe and caring schools are most effective when leadership is committed to applying the program at a schoolwide or district level to create systemic change. My thanks go to Dr. Wilfredo T. Laboy, superintendent of Lawrence Public Schools, and Dr. Mary Lou Bergeron, assistant superintendent of Lawrence Public Schools, for their foresight regarding the value of social and emotional learning in supporting students personally as well as academically. Dr. Bergeron has been particularly helpful in testing and proving this premise in schools.

Thanks to the staff at Free Spirit Publishing for their dedication to producing great products: to Publisher Judy Galbraith for her vision and belief in the power of the SCS program; to John Kober, editor, for his ongoing support, guidance, patience, and insight during the creation of the products; to Deb Anderson, editor, for her extraordinary ability to edit both from her teaching experience and her heart; and to the production team and all the others who pull all the pieces together to make a book.

Thanks to J Campbell at ArtVille, Inc., for his professionalism, creativity, and ability to bring the activity pages in this book to life. Also, thanks to my special educator friends, Kathy Kennedy Budge and Lynn Pauly, who listened, offered support, and used their ability to think outside the box to find the best way possible to connect with students.

This book series could not have been completed without the support of my wonderful family. My deepest gratitude goes to my husband, Steve Petersen, for the endless hours he worked by my side, for his ongoing encouragement, for his incredible creativity, and for urging me to always reach for excellence. My heartfelt appreciation also goes to my daughter, Alexia, for her patience and support during this project and for reminding me daily about the true meaning of parenting. Warm thanks go to my parents for their unconditional love, for teaching me to believe in myself, and for encouraging me to follow my dreams.

CONTENTS

FOREWORD

Dr. Katia Petersen has long been a champion for children and has dedicated her career to educating children and adults about the importance of social and emotional development in our youth and ourselves. Her vision, as a practitioner, has been to include life-skills education in the school day. She wants teachers to connect with students in a meaningful way and students to understand the relevance of school and how best to use it as a resource for self-development and well-being. Safe & Caring Schools is the culmination of more than 25 years of experience working in schools to help educators and others enhance the well-being and emotional literacy skills in children from preschool through high school.

In Safe & Caring Schools, Dr. Petersen has created a comprehensive approach to provide a solid foundation for infusing social and emotional literacy skills—including recognition of emotions, building relationships, conflict resolution, problem solving, decision making, and collaboration—into all areas of the program. The activities and resources provided in this book have been field-tested in classrooms across the United States with children from diverse backgrounds. Over the past years, I was fortunate enough to have worked with Dr. Petersen implementing Safe & Caring Schools in the Lawrence Public Schools. During the implementation, we collected a variety of data relative to overall school climate issues. In schools where Safe & Caring Schools was being implemented consistently, the data showed the following:

- an improvement in school climate
- greater parent engagement
- increased academic achievement
- a reduction in referrals for disciplinary infractions

We have continued to use the themes and activities of Safe & Caring Schools as a foundation for the social and emotional development of our students.

As an educator and school psychologist, I understand how children's levels of social and emotional literacy skill development impact their ability to succeed in school. I have seen firsthand how the development of these skills improved the overall academic and social success of our students. As an administrator, I am also acutely aware of the concerns that schools and school districts have relative to time on learning and adding new programs to the school day, especially at a time when there is a heightened focus on academic achievement and a demand for increased instructional time. With this in mind, Safe & Caring Schools was created to be an integrated component of systemic change at the classroom, school, and district levels. It has evolved into an easy-to-use, classroom-based approach that can be infused into all academic content areas with minimal effort on the part of teachers. The skills in the program are universal and can be addressed and reinforced throughout the school day and across grade levels. By infusing social and emotional learning across the curriculum, Safe & Caring Schools provides teachers with the flexibility and creativity they need to ensure students gain the skills they require to become successful students and members of society.

Mary Lou Bergeron, Ph.D.
Assistant Superintendent for
Operations and Support Services
Lawrence Public Schools
Lawrence, Massachusetts

PREFACE

Imagine a world where all children have an opportunity to learn and thrive—a safe place where adults help children become resilient. Imagine the impact safe and caring school communities can make in our challenging world as they encourage peer support, getting along, making ethical choices, problem solving, accountability, and cooperation. With this vision, I have created the Safe & Caring Schools (SCS) program to facilitate a blended curriculum of academic and social and emotional learning.

As times have changed, so have the demands put upon educators to meet the needs of every child. But one thing has never changed—the need for all children to feel appreciated, secure, and accepted. Many educators I speak to are concerned, and at times frustrated, about the lack of time to get everything done, the stress of how best to deal with challenging students, and the ever-growing issues of bullying and violence. Research increasingly supports that to reach the whole child, social and emotional learning (SEL) needs to be an integral part of the regular classroom curriculum. But, how much more can schools take on, what kind of support do they need, and how do they deal with the balancing act of mandated standards compliance and reaching children emotionally? SCS is a turnkey, literature-based program that supplies the school staff with a full suite of integrated materials to do this work, not as an add-on, but as part of the daily routine. Years of classroom testing have made Safe & Caring Schools a program that is easy to implement and sustain.

I've spent the past 27 years working in schools with staff and students of all ages, backgrounds, abilities, and talents. Using extensive feedback from thousands of educators, counselors, and parents, SCS addresses their needs by promoting social and emotional learning in the school, home, and community through the following:

- improving school climate and student behavior
- engaging and motivating students
- increasing academic achievement
- reducing stress
- increasing parent involvement
- enhancing staff teamwork

Time after time in testing this program, the schools that infused SEL into daily activities saw and felt a significant change in the behavior and language of their students. As attitudes and behaviors improved, so did academic performance. As teachers worked together making deliberate plans to embrace the SCS approach, they created systemic change in a natural way.

My hope is that the content and philosophy of this Safe & Caring Schools resource guide will inspire and help you enhance your role as a significant adult in your students' lives. I have created a tool that helps you use your wisdom, energy, and desire to reach every child on a personal and emotional level. Every day is a new adventure and an opportunity to create a better world for our children. As you work with SCS materials, I welcome your feedback, success stories, and suggestions for improvements. You can write to me in care of:

Free Spirit Publishing
217 Fifth Avenue North, Suite 200
Minneapolis, MN 55401
or email me at help4kids@freespirit.com

Katia S. Petersen, Ph.D.

PART 1

Skills for School.
Skills for Life.

The mission of the Safe & Caring Schools (SCS) program is to create sustainable, positive systemic change by infusing social and emotional learning (SEL) and character education into daily academic instruction from preschool through grade 8. This takes place in partnership with educators, counselors, administrators, parents, and community members to improve academic achievement and school climate.

"When you educate the whole child, you can count on academic growth as well, even if that's not the primary intent." These words from "The Whole Child," a 2007 report from the Association for Supervision and Curriculum Development, reinforce the value of social and emotional learning. SEL is no longer seen as an option to be taught separately from academics; rather, it can be taught and implemented in schools in a number of ways.

SCS supports the idea that reaching the hearts of children is equally as important as reaching their minds. As one teacher explains, "I have learned that if I want my students to succeed academically, I need to teach them how to listen, follow directions, communicate effectively, resolve problems, and make good choices."

Teaching kids life skills needs to become part of the daily routine. Learning to get along with others, accepting responsibility for one's own actions, and making better choices takes practice and needs the guidance and ongoing support from the adults in kids' lives. Consistency and repetition, as well as modeling desirable behaviors, will increase students' ability to internalize and use new skills in real-life situations.

Research Foundation

For several years now, there has been a growing body of scientifically-based research supporting the idea that enhanced social and emotional behaviors can have a strong impact on kids' success in school and, ultimately, in life (*Building Academic Success on Social and Emotional Learning: What Does the Research Say?* edited by Joseph E. Zins, Roger P. Weissberg, Margaret C. Wang, and Herbert J. Walberg. [New York: Teachers College Press, 2004]). The research substantiates that effective strategies for educational reform involve (1) a central focus on school climate change and (2) infusing SEL into regular academic lesson plans. Giving children a balance of intellectual and emotional instruction leads to more complete psychological development and helps them become better learners.

This approach is supported with hard data. For example: The Lucile Packard Foundation for Children's Health and the William T. Grant Foundation funded an analysis of 207 studies of social and emotional learning programs involving 288,000 elementary and secondary students from a cross section of urban, suburban, and rural schools. The results of the analysis are summarized in a 2008 report, "The Benefits of School-Based Social and Emotional Learning Programs" from CASEL (Collaborative for Academic, Social, and Emotional Learning). In evaluating academic outcomes, the study found that in schools where SEL is integrated into the regular programming, students scored 11 percentile points higher on standardized tests compared to students in schools not using an SEL program. Even though incorporating SEL activities required time in the school day, it did not negatively affect students' academic performance; rather, time spent on SEL improved academic performance. This project, conducted by Joseph A. Durlak of Loyola University in Chicago and Roger P. Weissberg at the University of Illinois at Chicago, was the first meta-analysis of research on the impact of SEL programs on students. Their full report is titled *The Effects of Social and Emotional Learning on the Behavior and Academic Performance of School Children*.

SCS incorporates a holistic approach in working with children, combining several research-based strategies into one program in order to nurture the whole child and promote student well-being. SCS defines student well-being as "the development of knowledge, attitudes, skills, and behaviors that maximize students' functioning in environments where they live and work—school, home, and community" (Romano, J. L. *Journal of Educational Research* 90, 1996). SCS provides you with a comprehensive set of core materials to enhance student well-being in a manner that is easily infused into your daily routine.

SCS materials incorporate a strengths-based approach that fosters resiliency in children to enable them to thrive and become successful in school and in life. Recent research shows that focusing on strengths is one of the key elements in supporting our youth, and schools play a critical role in the development of the strengths or assets in students.

- -

As Bonnie Benard writes in *Resiliency: What We Have Learned* (San Francisco: WestEd, 2004):

A framework, research support, and a rationale for resilience-based prevention and education include the following assumptions:

- Resilience is a capacity all youth have for healthy development and successful learning.
- Certain personal strengths are associated with healthy development and successful learning.
- Certain characteristics of families, schools, and communities are associated with the development of personal strengths and, in turn, healthy development and successful learning.
- Changing the life trajectories of children and youth from risk to resilience starts with changing the beliefs of the adults in their families, schools, and communities.

- -

SCS uses a complete and comprehensive plan that makes sense and works.

- It complements and enhances the well-being of children by promoting self-awareness, self-respect, integrity, and compassion to help them become productive citizens of any community.
- It encourages students to take risks and become active learners, regardless of their abilities, language barriers, or cultural differences.
- It leads students to make connections with the world around them by practicing the skills they need to face daily challenges.
- It allows students to realize their potential as positive leaders by providing social and emotional education as part of academic learning.

SCS activities support standards and comply with best practices for SEL infusion at school while providing opportunities for you, the teacher, to use your creativity. When aligned with the key competencies of the Collaborative for Academic, Social, and Emotional Learning (CASEL), the SCS activities clearly address those key SEL competencies: 1) awareness of self and others, 2) positive attitudes and values, 3) responsible decision making, and 4) social interaction skills.

These SCS materials have been tested with teachers and students of all abilities and backgrounds in public, private, city, and suburban schools. The program has been successful due to the commitment of staff, ongoing support from leadership, and awareness that all student needs—emotional, social, and intellectual—must be met. The schools that had the most success with the program developed strong relationships with their students by infusing SCS principles into the culture of the school, rather than just using occasional add-on SEL or character education units. At these schools, teachers brought the activities to life by modeling desirable behaviors and creating an environment where all students felt safe, accepted, recognized, and celebrated for their individuality every day.

A Schoolwide Commitment

To improve classroom and school climate, the SCS materials can be used by an individual teacher or by an entire school or district. Either approach will work, but a systemic change can be realized only when an entire school makes a commitment to become a safe and caring place. By choosing the schoolwide approach, a school has the benefit of teamwork and support from all staff, plus parents and community members. Through the common language of clear expectations, consistency of messages, modeling of desirable behavior, and the use of vocabulary that will help everyone communicate more effectively, you will be able to create positive systemic change in your school.

To implement a schoolwide SCS program:

- Include social and emotional learning in your mission statement.
- Establish clear expectations for positive behavior.
- Be consistent with expectations and consequences.
- Establish a yearlong plan to reinforce parent involvement.
- Create a support system for all students, staff, and parents.
- Coordinate communication among all staff, including teachers, specialists, administrators, counselors, support staff, substitute teachers, and aides.
- Plan opportunities to recognize and celebrate successes.

Although classroom teachers are the primary implementers of the SCS lessons, administrators, counselors, social workers, health teachers, and other staff can be actively involved in the effort to infuse SEL into all areas of the school. Creating a schoolwide program takes thought and planning, but it's well worth the effort.

"I think that it is not only our jobs as counselors, teachers, and administrators to help foster social skills, I think that it is absolutely the number one priority we need to be looking at right now. Having the Safe & Caring Schools program to help us do that makes our job that much easier."

COUNSELOR, ARLINGTON SCHOOL

PART 2

Content Overview

Students learn best when they see how what they are learning will impact their lives. The more your students can relate to a situation through experiential activities, the more interest they will show in the lesson and the easier it will be for them to apply the skills in real-life situations. This Safe & Caring Schools resource guide includes activities that enable students to have conversations, to learn through inquiry, and to feel empowered to change their own behavior and contribute to the creation of a positive classroom and school culture.

SCS MONTHLY THEMES

The SCS materials provide a sequenced, yet flexible program for social and emotional learning (SEL). Activities are grouped into nine units, one for each month of the typical school year. A theme is designated for each month of the year, so all grade levels using the program can focus on the same monthly theme. This allows each grade level in a schoolwide program to use its specific age-appropriate activities to support the common theme throughout the school. The SCS monthly themes are the following:

SEPTEMBER: Me and My Safe & Caring School

OCTOBER: Discovering Our Feelings

NOVEMBER: Caring People—My Support System

DECEMBER: Respect Yourself and Others

JANUARY: Caring About One Another—Bullying

FEBRUARY: Cooperation—Teaming Up for Success

MARCH: Getting Along with Others—Conflict Resolution

APRIL: The Power to Choose

MAY: Follow Your Dreams

Each SCS monthly theme is presented in a brief overview with key objectives to help focus the teaching. The theme is developed with a broad range of literature-based teaching activities, complete with reproducible activity sheets for the students. For easier printing of the activity sheets, they are available on the CD-ROM included with this book. See pages 14–15 for the "Year-at-a-Glance" chart of all the activities addressed within each monthly theme.

LITERATURE BASE

The SCS activities use children's literature to introduce key concepts, facilitate discussion, and lead into the activities. Using the books promotes active listening, helps increase comprehension, and motivates students to express themselves. The literature connections directly integrate SEL into core academics, making it easy for teachers to "build in" rather than "add on" SCS practices. Check your classroom, school library, or local public library for the books, or acquire some of the titles to start building an SEL library to share with all classrooms. When a suggested book is not available to you, consider another book of your own choosing or simply discuss the key concept of the book as it is described in the lesson plan.

LESSON PLANS

Each activity is presented with simple directions that include the "Learning Objectives," the "Materials Needed," and a four-part teaching plan: "**READ**," "**DISCUSS**," "**DO**," "**RELATE**." In "Read," a book related to the activity topic is suggested for shared reading. "Discuss" develops the topic through guided discussion of the book. "Do" provides instructions for using the lesson's activity and reproducible sheet. "Relate" offers ideas and discussion prompts to connect the topic to the students' daily lives; these ideas can be good writing prompts for journal entries.

The activities are designed to be used as starting points to introduce the key concepts of a safe and caring school. With open conversation, kids will gain a better understanding of the concepts and a sense of ownership of their own growth. See pages 14–15 for the "Year-at-a-Glance" chart of all the activities addressed within each monthly theme.

INTEGRATED ACTIVITIES

In addition to the more than 100 lesson plans, ideas for integrating each monthly theme across curricular areas—language arts, literature, social studies, art, music, and math—are provided to follow up and expand on topics.

ASSESSMENT

Best practices include ongoing assessment for program mastery. The final activity sheet for each month is a short quiz to assess the students' grasp of the concepts related to the monthly theme. Three types of questions and a writing activity are included. You may choose to use a quiz as a pre- and post-test to demonstrate where students started and how far they have grown by unit's end.

YEAR-ROUND ACTIVITIES

To support the success of a schoolwide effort, a set of activities that can be implemented at the start of the school year and used throughout the year is included (pages 8–10). These activities provide the school with a common vision and language that will maximize the benefits of the SCS program.

SCS Implementation Plan

The SCS activities have been successfully used in homerooms, regular classroom settings, during circle time, and as part of before- and after-school childcare and various youth or club programs.

Classroom teachers are commonly the primary implementers of the SCS lessons. Materials can be used independently in each classroom, but for systemic change, schools should consider a building-wide program. When all school staff—including teachers, administrators, counselors, social workers, media specialists, aides, coaches, support staff, and childcare providers—are involved in supporting the program, the students benefit from consistency of message and modeling of positive behavior. Schoolwide implementation creates an environment where students know what is expected of them, no matter where they are or what activities they are involved in throughout the day. To support the success of schoolwide implementation, it is essential for all staff to understand the philosophy of the SCS program—its goals, objectives, and action plan—and to be committed to working as a team to create a safe and caring school.

Counselors and social workers can use the program in small, student support groups during the school day, as part of after-school activities, or for parent presentations. In one-on-one situations, the activities can be used to practice specific skills, such as being assertive, using "I-messages," or defusing negative situations. In the testing of the SCS program, we have observed counselors and social workers playing a leadership role in promoting a comprehensive approach in the way SCS is used by all staff.

Media specialists and librarians have supported the schoolwide monthly theme by selecting appropriate reading and audiovisual materials for classes. Children can read the books alone, or the media specialist can have read-aloud sessions and discuss how the book's characters feel, express their emotions, deal with conflict, and resolve problems.

An SCS library corner can be set up so staff and students know which books support the theme of each month. Social studies, writing, and art teachers can provide support with SCS theme-based projects.

The Essential Role of Leadership

Children look to the adults around them for guidance, support, and safety. As the leaders of your school and classroom communities, you set the tone for the school year. To create a safe and caring school and achieve long-term positive change, the following strategies are recommended.

In a schoolwide program:

- **Mission.** Identify creating a safe and caring school as a schoolwide goal.

- **Core Team.** Assign a group to oversee the SCS program to keep implementation on track. The core team may be teachers from each grade level or a combination of teachers, administrators, support staff, specialists, and parents.

- **Action Plan.** Create and communicate an implementation plan to all staff, parents, and the community. Keep the lines of communication open so everyone has a voice.

- **Professional Development.** Use training and department planning to enhance the instructional process and effectively use new materials. Plan to train new teachers each year in the SCS program through in-service and teacher mentoring. Provide ongoing support, positive feedback, and a chance to celebrate progress.

- **Comprehensive Approach.** Fully integrate SEL into the daily curriculum and the daily lives of students and teachers.

In the classroom:

- **Clear Expectations.** Have students help you create the classroom rules. Their active involvement will lead to positive engagement.

- **Follow Through.** Let students know you are committed to making sure everyone feels safe and has the right to learn and enjoy being in your classroom. Following through shows them you mean what you say.

- **Connect with Each Child.** Get to know your students at the beginning of the year. This will help you build strong, trusting relationships. As you invest in them, they will invest in you.

- **No Tolerance.** Explain to students the meaning of no tolerance for violence, harassment, and negative behavior. Conflicts are a normal part of life, but bullying and harassing others in your safe and caring school are not.

Teaching Tips

There are no simple answers or quick fixes that will create the kind of school community you and your students will want to be a part of every day. But there are a number of things you can do to engage kids in the process of learning to get along with others and accepting responsibility for their own actions. Here are a few suggestions.

BEST PRACTICES

Because the SCS materials are group-graded, plan to meet regularly (at least monthly) with all the teachers using the same book to determine which activities everyone will use. You may want to use some activities at all grade levels to support the schoolwide program, while reserving others for a specific grade level. Keep in mind that some repetition of activities is a good thing because it aids in learning and reinforcing key concepts.

You can take several steps to help make the SCS program successful:

- Become familiar with the material. Review this resource guide in its entirety prior to using it.

- Be flexible. Use your creativity and knowledge to adapt the activities to meet the needs of your students.

- Be positive. Motivate and inspire your students.

- Diversify your teaching style. This SCS resource guide provides you with a diverse range of

activities that enable you to work with multiple learning styles.

- Develop a cohesive group of students. Use small groups and pairs of students to complete many of the activities. Vary the way groups are formed—try counting off; odd and even numbers; using colors of clothes, shoes, eyes, or hair; alphabetical order; height; letting students choose (be sensitive to problems of exclusion); or other creative ways.

When lessons have personal meaning to students, they are more likely to change their behavior because they want to, rather than because they are told to do so. To motivate your students and make the lessons personal, keep these best practices in mind:

- Help children understand the new skills and why they matter to them.

- Demonstrate what the new skills look like, sound like, and feel like.

- Create opportunities for children to practice their new skills.

- Consider the use of journal writing to help kids personalize their new skills.

- Use teachable moments to correct and redirect children.

- Celebrate the students who adopt desirable behaviors in school.

- Model the new social and emotional skills as often as possible.

- Infuse SEL into academic subject areas.

PARENT INVOLVEMENT

Involve parents and guardians in the SCS process. Once you establish your classroom and school expectations, send a copy of them to the parents and guardians of all students. Enclose a short letter explaining how the SCS program works in your classroom and school. Explain that you are actively teaching children social and emotional skills along with academics, and include the advantages of doing so. Ask for their support to help children practice the same expectations and skills at home for reinforcement and consistency.

Keep the parents actively involved throughout the year by maintaining open communication and creating opportunities for open communication.

- Establish a parent communication bulletin board where parents can easily pick up new information or drop off a note for you.
- Send home a monthly newsletter with tips, ideas, success stories, great books to read, projects and activities currently in progress, and pictures from events at your safe and caring school.
- Encourage parents to visit your classroom to help with specific activities, share information, or read books with the students.
- Display the Caring Hearts Tree (see page 9) so adults can see how many acts of kindness the children have demonstrated.
- Create Safe & Caring folders to keep students' completed work for parents to review often.
- Invite parents and family members to the Ambassadors of Peace celebrations (see page 8), and while recognizing their children note the support from home, too.

CIRCLE TIME

Misunderstandings at school, teasing, bullying, or use of inappropriate language can turn into big problems that take time away from your teaching. Be proactive by using classroom meetings (circle time) to address these issues. By doing so, you create a forum where students can share their feelings, as well as review, process, and discuss ways to positively resolve conflicts.

Circle time gives you the opportunity to get to know your students better and allows you to build stronger relationships. At the same time, students have the opportunity to practice listening, taking turns, sharing feelings, showing empathy for others, problem solving, and decision making. Explain to your students the purpose of circle time and establish clear expectations so students feel safe to participate. You may want to start with these instructions:

- Be a good listener.
- Wait for your turn to speak.
- Don't use put-downs.
- Respect everyone's feelings and ideas.
- It's okay to disagree.
- You have the right to pass.

Morning circle gives you a sense of how your students feel, which helps you set the tone for the day. Ask your students to share something that is happening in their lives. This is also a good time to review your expectations and give students a quick preview of the day's activities.

Midday circle works well for students who return from lunch, recess, or special events with complaints or hurt feelings. When these feelings are not addressed, they can contribute to the students' inability to focus on the learning activities.

End-of-the-day circle covers unfinished business, reviews the day, celebrates accomplishments, and reminds students that you look forward to seeing them the next day. Students who leave school feeling isolated, hurt, threatened, or bullied on a regular basis often choose to skip school. Providing a safe environment for sharing feelings and resolving conflicts in a timely fashion will help the students feel secure and ready to come back the next day. It takes only one caring adult to make a difference in a child's life.

Emergency circle gives you the time you need to confront issues as they happen so you can go back to teaching and students can complete their day without interference. The key is to be proactive and redirect your students before negative behaviors get out of control.

If students share too much personal information during meetings, explain the difference between private and public information. Take time to explain confidentiality and the importance of respecting each other's privacy. If a child refers to anything at home that sounds like an abusive situation, don't discuss it in class but bring it to the attention of a school counselor or administrator.

Below are a few tips for organizing and operating your circle time.

- Puppets make excellent vehicles to introduce new concepts and activities, leading group discussions, helping children with problem solving, reminding students of rules, and encouraging shy students. Let children use puppets to express their feelings or to role play situations. (See page 8 for more information on using puppets.)
- Popular song tunes are great audio cues to use to alert children that circle time is starting or ending. Try creating your own class theme song with the help of the children. You could also consider using a bell or triangle to signal the start or end of circle time. To encourage leadership and responsibility, have a different child each day or week be responsible for providing the bell or triangle signals.

- To give everyone equal time to share with the group, and to encourage shy children to speak, use a prop like a sponge ball. Pass the ball to a child and tell the group that the one holding the ball is the only one allowed to speak. The others are to be quiet listeners. If a child takes too long with sharing, gently take the ball away, thank the child, and pass the ball to someone else. At times you may want to use a directed activity for sharing. For example, pass the ball and say, "Share one positive thing that happened to you since yesterday." Other topics you may want to consider could include family activities, trips, favorite foods, favorite things to do alone or with others, and favorite movies. Let the children suggest sharing topics, too.

STORY TIME

Stories open up a world full of adventure and give children a chance to use their powers of imagination to gain new knowledge and skills. SCS uses great books in every lesson to introduce new concepts or reinforce the learning of skills, such as dealing with bullies, making friends, or making good choices. Read stories aloud to the students, have them do independent reading, let buddies read together, and find other creative ways to get kids engaged in the literature selections.

Stories, both the favorites and the unfamiliar, motivate children to read and express themselves. Use story time to promote active listening, increase comprehension, practice oral and written language, and help kids gain a sense of confidence and a feeling of accomplishment. As you help the students make the connection between the characters in the story and their personal lives, they will be learning new social and emotional skills.

PUPPETS

Puppets are a great tool for helping students discuss tough situations and identify and appropriately express their feelings and emotions. A puppet's style and "voice" can represent particular behaviors or feelings, such as happiness, sadness, excitement, anger, silliness, being demanding, shyness, assertiveness, or stuffiness. The more personality a puppet develops, the easier it will be for kids to identify with it and learn from it.

You can be as simple or as elaborate as you want in creating and using puppets. For more information, there are a number of websites and books about creating your own puppets and how best to use them in teaching.

Year-Round Activities

You will want to implement some or all of these ideas and yearlong activities to build a positive school climate and create a safe and caring community for staff, students, and parents. Implementing these ideas at the start of the year and continuing to use them throughout the school year will support the common SCS vision, language, and expectations.

TEN IDEAS THAT WORK

1. Use grade level or department meetings to review expectations, rules, and support resources, and to discuss other topics related to SCS implementation.
2. Provide a monthly Ambassadors of Peace celebration (see below).
3. Decorate hallways and bulletin boards to promote your safe and caring school. Each month have a designated classroom display some of its completed activities.
4. Use morning announcements to communicate monthly themes and the monthly vocabulary (see first activity of each month).
5. In a parent newsletter, include the monthly theme with tips and ideas for home and family use.
6. Reinforce Safe & Caring Schools principles by displaying the SCS posters (available separately, see page 193) in classrooms and throughout the school in common areas.
7. Have books related to the SCS themes featured in the library or classrooms.
8. Involve the student council or other student groups in promoting the messages of being a safe and caring school.
9. Use peer teaching by having older students teach monthly activities to younger students through reading, writing, drama, or art.
10. Include school nurses, health teachers, and other school resource staff in promoting safe and healthy choices.

AMBASSADORS OF PEACE

The "How to Be an Ambassador of Peace" activity (page 24) recognizes students for making good choices, resolving conflicts in peaceful ways, and practicing their positive character skills. Use the Ambassadors of Peace poster to remind students of the skills they need to work on to support a safe and caring school.

To conclude each month's SCS activities, nominate one or two students per classroom as Ambassadors of Peace for practicing their skills of peacemaking, such as making good choices, being respectful, or helping others. Have classroom teachers, counselors, or students nominate students by describing their specific peacemaking attributes. Create an Ambassadors of Peace nomination form using this model.

Plan an Ambassadors of Peace celebration, which might be a classroom party, a schoolwide or department assembly, or a grade-level breakfast. Invite each nominee's family to attend the celebration. Follow up with phone calls to encourage parents, other family members, or friends to attend.

During the celebration, present the children with Ambassadors of Peace certificates, buttons, or pendants. Give parents the nomination forms so they know why their children were chosen as Ambassadors of Peace. (For example, Marina is an excellent listener, a great friend, and is helpful and respectful to everyone.)

You may choose to acknowledge the Ambassadors of Peace on the same day as a "Student of the Month" celebration. This coordinates the two programs into an existing initiative, which may be easier than finding time for separate events in a busy school calendar.

SAFE & CARING SCHOOLS
SKILLS FOR SCHOOL. SKILLS FOR LIFE.
AMBASSADOR OF PEACE NOMINATION

Date_____

I nominate _____

as an Ambassador of Peace because _____

_____

_____ .

Signed_____

CARING HEARTS
Catching kids doing the right thing and highlighting the positive behavior you see will motivate students to change negative behavior. Give children paper hearts each time they are caught using positive character skills, such as showing kindness, sharing, working together, or making good choices.

One option is to hand out the hearts every day and then collect them at the end of the week. Create a "Caring Hearts Tree" on a wall or door. Add the hearts to it each week, so children can see how often they use their new skills. The goal is to create an environment where all children have an opportunity to be recognized and to celebrate positive change. Encourage parent volunteers to help you cut out as many hearts as possible so they are available to you at all times.

Remember that each day is a new beginning and another chance to succeed at learning something new. Hearts are not to be taken away if a student makes a bad choice. Redirecting behavior and giving students a reminder of what is needed to earn a heart will teach responsibility for one's actions.

COMMUNITY PEACE GARDEN
To practice teamwork skills, listening to and following directions, and taking responsibility, involve the students, parents, and community in creating a garden. The peace garden can be a place where individuals or groups go when they need a quiet moment or need to resolve an issue before it becomes a big conflict. This is a good project in which to involve parents, community volunteers, gardeners, garden shops, carpenters, and home supply stores for donated time, expertise, and materials.

Choose a spot—outside, inside, or both—for your garden. (If inside, use potted plants and indoor benches or chairs in the garden.) With some expert help, build wooden benches to place in the garden. Prepare the soil for planting. When it is ready, plant flowers, bulbs, trees, and shrubs. Decorate the area with rocks, and have the children paint words of peace on the rocks. (You could use words and phrases from the SCS themes.) Add posts in the garden that can be used to display the children's artwork during the year. As you work together on the garden, reinforce lessons of teamwork, cooperation, responsibility, caring, and nurturing. Don't forget to have a community celebration once your garden is complete. Work together to provide ongoing care for the garden.

PEACE RUGS

Children can use carpet squares, which you can call "Peace Rugs," as the setting to resolve conflicts in peaceful ways. After you model the steps of resolving a conflict without hurting the other person physically or emotionally (see activities for March), give students opportunities to practice using role-play situations. When real conflicts arise, students will be able to use this process on their own without disrupting the class. It might take longer for some students than others to understand that they can resolve conflicts together, but it is worth the effort to get to that point. No matter how big or small the conflicts that students face daily, the skills of problem solving and decision making are ones they will use for a lifetime.

The process starts with kids sitting on their peace rugs face-to-face. Have them take turns sharing responses to these questions: What's the problem? How do I feel about it? What choices do I have? What can I do to make things better? You will need to direct these discussions at first to help the children get comfortable with this process. When students are done talking and reach an agreement on what to do, have them shake hands or give a high five. Make sure to follow up with them later to see if the plan is working.

FEELINGS MAILBOX

Create a classroom mailbox and label it "Feelings Mailbox." With all you try to accomplish during the day, it is not always possible to recognize the emotions and address the concerns of your students in a timely manner. The feelings mailbox is a safe place where students can leave confidential messages for you when they need adult support. Go through the box daily so you can decide the urgency and the type of support a student needs.

> *"The Safe & Caring Schools materials are infused right along with the curriculum being studied in the classrooms. It is not an extra, not something above and beyond."*
>
> ASSISTANT PRINCIPAL—SOUTH LAWRENCE EAST SCHOOL

SCS Teacher Survey

Use the teacher survey on the next pages at the beginning of the school year, during the year when you want to check your progress, and as a post-test at the end of the school year. Part 1 helps you monitor your inclusion of social and emotional learning in your routine. Part 2 helps you understand how safe students feel in school and if they use their social and emotional skills on a regular basis.

SKILLS FOR SCHOOL. SKILLS FOR LIFE.

TEACHER SURVEY—PART 1
SCHOOL/CLASSROOM CLIMATE

Using the 1 to 5 scale, circle the response that best describes your actions and proficiency at this time.
1 = Consistently   2 = Often   3 = Occasionally   4 = Infrequently   5 = Never

1. I set clear expectations in my classroom.	1	2	3	4	5
2. I enforce classroom and schoolwide expectations.	1	2	3	4	5
3. I teach students about being accountable for their own actions.	1	2	3	4	5
4. I recognize my students for using their social and emotional skills by choosing them as Ambassadors of Peace.	1	2	3	4	5
5. I develop a sense of community in my classroom.	1	2	3	4	5
6. I use circle time/classroom meetings to review new ideas and to practice social and emotional literacy.	1	2	3	4	5
7. I use cooperative groups to reinforce teamwork and peer teaching.	1	2	3	4	5
8. I model and use teachable moments to reinforce social and emotional learning in the lessons I teach.	1	2	3	4	5
9. I teach social and emotional literacy by infusing activities from the Safe & Caring Schools resource guide.	1	2	3	4	5
10. I teach students strategies to help them deal with bullying behavior.	1	2	3	4	5
11. I teach students conflict resolution and problem-solving strategies.	1	2	3	4	5
12. I meet with other staff to discuss and plan schoolwide activities to reinforce social and emotional learning.	1	2	3	4	5
13. I seek support from my colleagues when problems arise in my classroom so I can solve them more effectively.	1	2	3	4	5
14. I assess the effectiveness of my efforts to include social and emotional learning in my daily teaching practice.	1	2	3	4	5
15. I connect with parents to be partners in teaching and supporting social and emotional learning at home as in school.	1	2	3	4	5

SKILLS FOR SCHOOL. SKILLS FOR LIFE.

TEACHER SURVEY—PART 2
SKILLS AND KNOWLEDGE

Using the 1 to 5 scale, circle the response that best describes your actions and proficiency at this time.
1 = Consistently   2 = Often   3 = Occasionally   4 = Infrequently   5 = Never

1. My students feel safe at school.	1	2	3	4	5
2. My students understand the school and classroom expectations.	1	2	3	4	5
3. My students follow the school and classroom expectations.	1	2	3	4	5
4. My students know how to ask for help.	1	2	3	4	5
5. My students use conflict-resolution skills to deal with problems.	1	2	3	4	5
6. My students identify and express their emotions appropriately.	1	2	3	4	5
7. My students use good manners.	1	2	3	4	5
8. My students show respect toward adults and children.	1	2	3	4	5
9. My students show empathy toward others.	1	2	3	4	5
10. My students appropriately deal with bullying behavior at school.	1	2	3	4	5
11. My students practice active listening.	1	2	3	4	5
12. My students demonstrate the ability to make good choices.	1	2	3	4	5
13. My students recognize their gifts and talents.	1	2	3	4	5
14. My students know how to set goals.	1	2	3	4	5
15. My students have positive dreams for the future.	1	2	3	4	5

PART 3

Year-at-a-Glance, Grades 1–2

Use the chart on pages 14–15 as a planning tool to review the SCS concepts and topics for the school year. You will see that the activities support the monthly theme and there is a logical progression to the order of the themes. Of course, it is possible to adjust the order of the themes to better fit with your curriculum or with other schoolwide events. Be creative with your planning and teaching.

Along with your teaching colleagues, select the activities you will use in your classroom each month. For example, you may decide that each 1st-grade teacher will devote 30 minutes to the same activity on the same day or within the same week. Since this is a group-graded resource guide, be sure you are involving all the appropriate teachers in the planning.

Also, you can use the year-at-a-glance chart to help you plan ahead to gather the books you want to use as the literature base for each lesson. The suggested book for each activity is listed opposite the activity name. See the activity directions for additional literature suggestions.

> *"In our plan we are focused on literacy and writing, and we are integrating the Safe & Caring Schools materials with literacy and writing. It has been effective, encourages our children, and has parent support."*
>
> **PRINCIPAL—WETHERBEE SCHOOL**

Year-at-a-Glance, Grades 1–2

THEME	ACTIVITY TITLE—LITERATURE CONNECTION	
September Me and My Safe & Caring School	SCS Vocabulary Builder Safe & Caring Promise—*The Quilt* Safe & Caring Quilt—*The Name Quilt* Safe & Caring Rules—*Officer Buckle and Gloria* The Golden Rule—*Michael's Golden Rules* Getting to Know You—*But Not Kate*	There's Only One of Me!—*Why Am I Different?* Discover Your Name—*Chrysanthemum* My Family Book—*The Family Book* Can I Play?—*Feeling Left Out* How to Be an Ambassador of Peace—*The Peace Book* Comprehension Quiz
October Discovering Our Feelings	SCS Vocabulary Builder Feelings Soup—*Smile-A-Saurus!* Feelings Musical Chairs—*The Way I Feel* I Feel—*Matthew and Tilly* Bugs in a Row—*The Grouchy Ladybug*	Catch That Feeling—*Glad Monster, Sad Monster* What Happens When I Get Angry?—*When I Feel Angry* Stop, Think, Choose—*Franklin's Bad Day* I-Message—*Ruby the Copycat* Safe & Caring Hearts—*I Can't Wait* Comprehension Quiz
November Caring People— My Support System	SCS Vocabulary Builder People Who Care About Me—*Spinky Sulks* The Safe Thing to Do—*I Can Be Safe* The Helper in Me—*Amos & Boris* What Is a Friend?—*The Best Friends Book*	My Friend and I Can . . .—*We Are Best Friends* Friendship Rainbow—*A Rainbow of Friends* Warm Thank You—*The Mitten Tree* Wonder About Worries—*Wemberly Worried* Good Helpers—*The Lion and the Mouse* Comprehension Quiz
December Respect Yourself and Others	SCS Vocabulary Builder I Respect Others—*I'm Like You, You're Like Me* Practice Your Manners—*Mind Your Manners: In School* Good Manners or Bad Manners—*It's a Spoon, Not a Shovel* Don't Put Up with Put-Downs—*Whoopi's Big Book of Manners* Thumbs Up or Thumbs Down—*Talk and Work It Out*	Good Manners Flower—*Please Say Please! Penguin's Guide to Manners* Kind Hand—*Hands Are Not for Hitting* I Did Not Do It!—*It Wasn't My Fault* Playing Fair—*Join In and Play* It's the Truth—*I'm Telling the Truth: A First Look at Honesty* Let's Be Honest—*Jamaica and the Substitute Teacher* Comprehension Quiz

January Caring About One Another—Bullying	SCS Vocabulary Builder People Packages—*Different Just Like Me* What Is Bullying?—*Being Bullied* Different but the Same—*All the Colors of the Earth* Bully Problems—*King of the Playground* What to Do About Being Bossy—*Bootsie Barker Bites*	Stop the Tease Monster Game—*Oliver Button Is a Sissy* Tattling or Telling?—*Don't Squeal Unless It's a Big Deal* Caring Takes Courage—*Believing Sophie* What Can I Do About Bullies?—*Loudmouth George and the Sixth-Grade Bully* SCS Ambassadors of Peace—*The Recess Queen* Comprehension Quiz
February Cooperation—Teaming Up for Success	SCS Vocabulary Builder That's What I Like About You—*Rosie and Michael* Secret Gift—*When I Care About Others* I Am Responsible—*The Little Red Hen* Responsibility Zones—*Heartprints*	Team Puzzles—*The Doorbell Rang* School of Sharing Fish—*The Rainbow Fish* Apology Accepted—*Lilly's Purple Plastic Purse* Working Together—*Working Together* Trust Is Golden—*Jack and the Beanstalk* Comprehension Quiz
March Getting Along with Others—Conflict Resolution	SCS Vocabulary Builder I Am a Good Listener—*Listen, Buddy* Good Listening—*Sing, Sophie!* Listening Journal—*The Listening Walk* My Anger Button—*Stop Picking on Me*	Better Way to Say It—*I Want It* Conflict Cartoons—*Stephanie's Ponytail* What's the Problem?—*The Owl and the Woodpecker* Safe & Caring Ways to Solve Problems—*Katharine's Doll* Do the Right Thing—*Noisy Nora* Comprehension Quiz
April The Power to Choose	SCS Vocabulary Builder My Choices—*My Big Lie* Positive Choice!—*Shrinking Violet* What Could Happen?—*Me First* Good Friends, Tough Choices—*A Weekend with Wendell*	Author for a Day—*Lilly's Big Day* Give and Take—*Click, Clack, Moo: Cows That Type* Choosing to Be Responsible—*It's Not Fair!* Safe & Caring Sun—*Jamaica's Blue Marker* Growing Responsibility—*Jason Takes Responsibility* Comprehension Quiz
May Follow Your Dreams	SCS Vocabulary Builder My Gifts and Talents—*Willa the Wonderful* What's My Job?—*Matthew's Dream* When I Grow Up, I Want to Be...—*When I Grow Up* Working on a Dream—*Brave Irene*	Climbing High!—*The Little Red Ant and the Great Big Crumb* I Am a Star—*Stand Tall, Molly Lou Melon* Looking Up to My Hero—*If Only I Could!* My Book About Practice—*Ronald Morgan Goes to Bat* My Great Year!—*Emily's Art* Comprehension Quiz

"In preparation for becoming a teacher, I learned a lot about effective teaching methods, ways to build reading skills, and how to boost test scores. But one thing I really wasn't prepared for were all the other needs the students have that need to be met before they can become active learners—kids' social needs, playing the role of parent, and taking care of emotional issues and crises that come up. It's really important that students have that emotional security before they can become good learners. Without that, teaching is really going to be ineffective. The Safe & Caring Schools program has helped me bring that support into the learning process in a natural way while keeping the academic work moving forward."

TEACHER—WETHERBEE SCHOOL

SKILLS FOR SCHOOL. SKILLS FOR LIFE.

SEPTEMBER
Me and My Safe & Caring School

- **Setting Expectations**
- **Classroom Community**
- **Social Awareness**
- **Self-Awareness and Acceptance**
- **Belonging**

Children grow strong when they receive unconditional love, ongoing support, and positive recognition. Before we can begin to teach them about getting along, solving problems peacefully, making good choices, and making friends, we need to help them understand the amazing journey of self-discovery they can have at school. To learn to care for others, children first have to learn to care for themselves.

MONTHLY OBJECTIVES
Students will:

- learn about and participate in setting up a safe and caring classroom community
- understand they are unique and learn to recognize, empathize with, and respect the individuality and diversity of others
- experience the importance of inclusion, belonging, and celebrating their families

TEACHING TIPS

- Setting clear expectations and teaching students how to interact with one another are the first steps to learning how to get along.
- It is essential to define the desirable and expected behaviors of your students.
- Students thrive when they know that who they are, what they say, and what they do matters to their teacher. Recognize them for their efforts to do well academically and socially.

SEPTEMBER INTEGRATED ACTIVITIES

In addition to the specific lesson plans for this month, you can use these optional ideas to integrate and extend the Safe & Caring themes into daily routines and across the curricular areas.

LANGUAGE ARTS

- Review and define the key words and phrases of the "Safe & Caring Rules" activity sheet: *safe, respect, bully free, share our feelings, agree, disagree, ask for help,* and *learn.* Play Simon Says using the words and the concepts they represent, for example, *Simon says all students who know how to ask for help take one step forward.*

- Write key words on the board from the "Safe & Caring Rules," "The Golden Rule," and "Safe & Caring Promise" activity sheets. Explain what the words mean, and then have the students help you complete sentences by providing the missing key words, for example, *In our safe and caring school we treat others with _____.*

LITERATURE

- Read *On the Town: A Community Adventure* by Judith Caseley. A boy and his mother keep track of people and places in their town to learn about their community. Have students share personal experiences of how it feels to be part of a community.

- Read *I Like Being Me* by Judy Lalli, and ask children to draw pictures of their favorite parts of the story. Share the pictures during circle time, and display them during the month of September.

- Read *How Do I Stand in Your Shoes* by Susan Debell. Miranda learns the true meaning of empathy after her teacher asks her to be more understanding with her classmates.

SOCIAL STUDIES

- The United Nations designated September 21 as Peace Day. Draw pictures and write short stories about what peace means. Read excerpts from *Make Someone Smile* by Judy Lalli.

ART

- Read *Sadako and the Thousand Paper Cranes* by Eleanor Coerr. It may take several days to finish the story. Sadako, a Japanese girl with leukemia, becomes a hero by trying to make 1,000 paper cranes. Make origami cranes with the students and hang them around the room. It could be a schoolwide activity to make 1,000 cranes.

- Read *Pablo Picasso: Breaking All the Rules* by True Kelley. Students can paint their own masterpieces after you review how Picasso followed his own rules to create unique artwork.

- Create "Welcome to Our School" cards for new students.

- Use the monthly theme to generate ideas for students to decorate a classroom bulletin board or door.

MUSIC

- Listen to songs on the *Free to Be . . . You and Me* CD by Marlo Thomas and Friends (www.freetobefoundation.org). Many of the songs pertain to the themes of this month. Discuss the lyrics with children and what the songs mean to them.

- Involve the students in identifying other favorite songs that reinforce safe and caring themes.

MATH

- Have students compare similar and different features or likes and dislikes of the class. You might say, "Let's count how many of our friends have curly hair. How many girls are in the room? How many boys are in the room? How many like ice cream? How many like to read?" Collect and record data as children raise their hands. Make graphs with the data.

- Read *The Quilting Bee* by Gail Gibbons to explore colors, shapes, and how people can work together to create beautiful quilts. Have students work in small groups to create simple paper quilts.

Safe & Caring Schools Vocabulary Builder

LEARNING OBJECTIVES

Students will:

- be introduced to vocabulary that supports learning how to behave in a safe and caring classroom
- internalize the vocabulary as they use it throughout the month and year in real-life situations

MATERIALS NEEDED

Pencils or pens, "Safe & Caring Vocabulary Builder" activity sheet (page 25)

LESSON PLAN

Use the vocabulary activities to introduce the concepts and common language associated with this month's theme. Throughout the month, use the words in writing, spelling, storytelling, and dealing with conflict situations. Add the words to your word wall.

For the Word Find activity, choose to use the key words, challenge words, or both. Discuss what the words mean after completing the page. You may want students to work in pairs to help each other.

For the fill-in-the-blanks activity, students add the missing letters to spell the words, which are also used in the word find *(safe, caring, promise, kind, rules, help)*.

Safe & Caring Promise

LEARNING OBJECTIVES

Students will:

- learn the meaning of a promise
- learn how to make a commitment to working together to help create a safe and caring school

MATERIALS NEEDED

The book *The Quilt* by Ann Jonas, "Safe & Caring Promise" miniposter (page 26), white paper, pencils, and markers or crayons

LESSON PLAN

READ *The Quilt*. This is a tale about an African-American girl's quilt that springs to life as she remembers the history of each piece of fabric.

> An optional text for further study is *The Class Trip* by Grace Maccarone. Sam has quite a scare when he gets separated from his group on a trip to the zoo. Sam learns an important lesson about protecting himself.

DISCUSS Ask students if they know what a promise means and discuss why promises are hard to keep sometimes. Ask them to share a time when they have made promises. Have each child draw a picture of something they promise they will do to have a caring classroom. Use the pictures to create a book about promises.

DO the "Safe & Caring Promise" miniposter activity. Read the Promise aloud and discuss the meaning of the words. Read it a second time, one line at a time, and have children repeat the lines after you. Have children sign their names, or first initials, on the poster to signify it is their promise.

RELATE the Safe & Caring Promise to the students' school lives. Explain that you will read the promise throughout the year to help everyone remember his or her promise to get along. Morning circle time is a good time to read the promise and set the tone for the day.

Safe & Caring Quilt

LEARNING OBJECTIVES

Students will:

- learn to work as members of a team
- review the Safe & Caring Promise

MATERIALS NEEDED

The book *The Name Quilt* by Phyllis Root, construction paper, butcher paper, a copy of the signed "Safe & Caring Promise" miniposter from the previous activity, glue, and markers, crayons, or paints

LESSON PLAN

READ   *The Name Quilt.* Sadie learns about the importance of family and belonging when her grandmother shares stories related to family members named on her quilt.

> An optional text for teacher shared reading is *The Colors of Us* by Karen Katz. Lena discovers that she and her friends and neighbors are all beautiful shades of brown.

DISCUSS   the importance of being part of a family; everyone needs to feel they belong. Ask the children how Sadie felt when the wind took the quilt away. What did Grandma do to help her feel better?

DO   Talk about different types of quilts, such as story quilts, pattern quilts, and special image quilts. (See *Quilting Across the Curriculum* by Wendy Buchberg.)

Distribute markers, crayons, or paints and construction paper cut into uniform squares. Ask the children to create pictures of how they can help make their school a safe and caring place. Be sure to add the students' names to the front of their squares. Assist children in gluing the individual squares on butcher paper around the "Safe & Caring Promise" miniposter to make a large classroom quilt. You may want to use a digital camera to take a picture of each child to display on the quilt's border or in the center of each child's square. Have students sign their pictures.

RELATE   the story you read to the quilt the students made in class. Tell students that each child has a story to tell and a place in the classroom community. Display the class quilt in a place where children and visitors can see it as a reminder that they are in a safe and caring school. As a group, brainstorm ideas of the little things everyone can do to make the classroom a fun place for learning with their friends.

Safe & Caring Rules

LEARNING OBJECTIVES

Students will:

- understand the importance of having and following rules
- learn what behaviors are expected of them and help create the rules for their classroom

MATERIALS NEEDED

The book *Officer Buckle and Gloria* by Peggy Rathmann, "Safe & Caring Rules" miniposter (page 27), and puppets (optional)

LESSON PLAN

READ   *Officer Buckle and Gloria.* Gloria, the police dog, saves the day by entertaining the children while Officer Buckle teaches them about rules.

> An optional text for teacher shared reading is *Second Grade Rules, Amber Brown* by Paula Danziger. Amber really wants a clean desk award, but no matter what she does her desk is always messy.

DISCUSS   Define the word *rule* and explain why we need rules in our lives.

Help children think about the kind of classroom they would like to be a part of all year (*fun, peaceful, safe, respectful, kind*).

DO   Review the "Safe & Caring Rules" miniposter. Using puppets or role-play, illustrate different situations that show how to follow the rules. (For example, "What would using kind words sound like, feel like, and look like?")

RELATE   the "Safe & Caring Rules" miniposter to classroom life. Post it where children can see it daily. Review the rules during teachable moments to make an application to real-life experiences. Remember to set clear expectations and reinforce them daily. Help students learn how to interact with others in positive ways.

The Golden Rule

LEARNING OBJECTIVES

Students will:

- learn the meaning of the golden rule
- apply the golden rule by treating others with kindness and respect

MATERIALS NEEDED

The book *Michael's Golden Rules* by Deloris Jordan and Roslyn M. Jordan, "Golden Rule" miniposter (page 28), "The Golden Rule" activity sheet (page 29), pencils or pens, and crayons or markers

LESSON PLAN

READ *Michael's Golden Rules*. Michael's best friend, Jonathan, strikes out at the end of a little league game, and his team loses. Walking home with the boys, Michael's uncle utters the well-known phrase that there is "a lot more to a game than winning or losing."

An optional text for teacher shared reading is *Angel Child, Dragon Child* by Michele Maria Surat. Ut, a Vietnamese girl attending school in the United States, misses her mother in Vietnam. Ut makes a new friend who presents her with a wonderful gift.

DISCUSS and read aloud the "Golden Rule" miniposter. Refer to the story you read to help students make the connection between respect and the golden rule. Why is it such an important rule? *(Because it helps us get along.)* Ask children if they think the golden rule helped Jonathon in the story. How would they feel if they were in the same situation? Brainstorm ways the children can practice using the golden rule.

DO "The Golden Rule" activity sheet. Ask children to draw a picture or write about a time when they were kind to someone and a time when someone was kind to them.

RELATE the kids' golden rule pictures or stories to daily activities at school. Collect the pictures and create an "Our Golden Rule" classroom book.

Getting to Know You

LEARNING OBJECTIVES

Students will:

- discover positive ways to make friends
- learn how to introduce themselves and get to know others

MATERIALS NEEDED

The book *But Not Kate* by Marissa Moss, "Getting to Know You" activity sheet (page 30), and pencils or pens

LESSON PLAN

READ *But Not Kate*. Little mouse Kate doesn't feel she's the best at anything or is special in any way. She feels so ordinary and so unspectacular—until the school magic show. Kate overcomes her shrinking-violet feelings when she discovers her own unique talents.

An optional text for teacher shared reading is *The Brand New Kid* by Katie Couric. Lazlo is a new kid in class who is teased and excluded from the first day. Eventually, Ellie begins to wonder what it must be like to be the new kid. She decides to get to know him, even at the risk of facing her friends' ridicule.

DISCUSS Why is it important to get to know each other? What does it feel like to meet new friends and become a member of a group? What can we do to help each other feel welcome in a group?

DO the "Getting to Know You" activity sheet. Choose one of these options to complete the activity.

- Have all members of the class move around the room and introduce themselves to others. Have each child complete the sheet by saying her or his name to a classmate and then checking if the classmate matches one of the items on the sheet. If there is a match, the student circles the item and writes the new friend's name beside it. Children work to find a new friend for each item.

- The teacher, or one student, announces the items on the sheet (one at a time) and asks the students to stand if it applies to them. Ask students to look around the room to see who else likes the same things.

RELATE   what the children learned about each other to what they can do when they meet someone new. Put the children into groups of two, preferably pairs that do not know each other very well. Have the two students introduce themselves and find at least one thing they have in common. After a few minutes, have the pairs introduce each other to the large group *(for example, My name is ____, and today I met ____. We both like ____.)*. Remind the children that one of the first steps to getting along is getting to know their friends in the classroom.

There's Only One of Me!

LEARNING OBJECTIVES
Students will:

- learn to appreciate their uniqueness
- work on accepting and appreciating the individuality in others

MATERIALS NEEDED

The book *Why Am I Different?* by Norma Simon and Dora Leder, "There's Only One of Me!" activity sheet (page 31), posterboard, pencils or pens, and crayons or markers

LESSON PLAN

READ   *Why Am I Different?* This book helps children see the ways they are "different" in family life and their personal preferences. They decide that being different is all right.

An optional text for teacher shared reading is *Nappy Hair* by Carolivia Herron. At a family picnic, everyone pokes fun at the youngest girl's nappy hair and wonders why it is that way. The answers involve African origins and pride in one's self.

DISCUSS   what it means to be special or unique. Review the importance of uniqueness and invite the children to name ways each of them is unique. Help them see that being an artist or a dancer, or liking to ride a bike or to sing, can make them unique. Explain that although they have differences, in many ways, they are still the same *(all have hair, eyes, mouth, families, friends)*.

DO   the "There's Only One of Me!" activity sheet. Ask the children to draw a picture of themselves. Encourage them to pay close attention to their special features, including eye color, facial features, type of hair, and glasses.

RELATE   how our similarities bring us together, but it is our differences that make us special. In circle time, share the kids' similarities and differences using their completed pictures. Note that similarities and differences are not only on the outside, but also on the inside. Have children share what they think makes them special on the inside. As an option, create a "We Are All Special" classroom book. Those who are able may write a short story about their uniqueness, including what they like and dislike, what matters to them, and the things they appreciate in others.

Discover Your Name

LEARNING OBJECTIVES
Students will:

- understand the importance and the meaning of their names
- learn each other's names, especially the new kids in class

MATERIALS NEEDED

The book *Chrysanthemum* by Kevin Henkes, "Discover Your Name" activity sheet (page 32), a name reference book such as *The Very Best Baby Name Book in the Whole Wide World* by Bruce Lansky, pencils or pens, and crayons or markers

LESSON PLAN

READ   *Chrysanthemum.* Chrysanthemum loves her name, until she starts school. On her first day of school, she is teased because she is named after a flower. When the students are introduced to their music teacher, Mrs. Delphinium Twinkle, everything changes.

An optional reading for teacher shared reading is *The Other Emily* by Gibbs Davis. Emily believes her name belongs to her alone, but on the first day of school she discovers she is not the only Emily in the world.

DISCUSS   Did Chrysanthemum like her name? What did her name mean? How did the children treat her on the first day of school? Were they kind and respectful to her? How did the teacher help Chrysanthemum? What happens at the end of the story?

DO   the "Discover Your Name" activity sheet. Each child writes his or her name on an activity sheet (help as needed). Then direct them to decorate around the names, encouraging them to use several of their favorite colors. Help the kids find the meaning of their names using the name reference book. Add that information to the activity sheet. A fun option is to write the meaning of each name on the activity sheets before class and let kids try to guess what sheet is theirs. Another option is to have students take the sheets home and have their families fill in the meaning of the names. Because some foreign names may be hard to find in name books, you may want to try using the Internet.

RELATE   to the class that each child's name is special and is something to be proud of. Have each child read her or his name aloud and show the completed activity sheet. Share the meaning of the names with the class.

My Family Book

LEARNING OBJECTIVES

Students will:

- explore the importance of families and how families differ
- celebrate being part of their families

MATERIALS NEEDED

The book *The Family Book* by Todd Parr, "My Family Book" activity sheet (page 33), and pencils or pens

LESSON PLAN

READ   *The Family Book*. The author celebrates many different types of families, all in a funny, yet reassuring, way that helps children understand the importance of belonging.

> An optional text for teacher shared reading is *All Families Are Special* by Norma Simon. When a teacher asks her students to talk about their families, each child speaks of a different configuration (a mom and dad, grandparents, or stepparents). The kids mention adoption, divorce, and the death of a parent and pets and discuss the good and bad times that families have together.

DISCUSS   the importance of being part of a family and how it feels to belong in a family. Explain that families do not have to be made up of relatives. What people refer to as a family often differs because of the given circumstances or the culture.

DO   the "My Family Book" activity sheet, helping the children understand what to do with each page and how to fold the pages to make a book. Be sensitive to adopted children who may or may not know any details about their families of origin. Have them focus on the members of their adoptive family. As an option, you may want to make an overhead transparency of the questions and do this as a group activity.

RELATE   what the children learned about different families to their own lives. Share the "Family Books" during circle time. Discuss similarities and differences among families.

Can I Play?

LEARNING OBJECTIVES

Students will:

- learn to ask to join activities in a respectful way
- practice, through role play, the steps of asking to join an activity

MATERIALS NEEDED

The book *Feeling Left Out* by Kate Petty and Charlotte Firmin, "Can I Play?" activity sheet (page 34), pencils or pens, and poster board

LESSON PLAN

READ   *Feeling Left Out*. New to the neighborhood, Chris feels left out of various activities until he learns new ways to make friends.

> An optional text for teacher shared reading is *Join In and Play* by Cheri J. Meiners. This book teaches the basics of cooperation, getting along, making friends, and being a friend. It includes ideas for games to use with kids to reinforce the skills being taught.

DISCUSS   how it feels to be left out. Discuss what they can do to include each other. Role-play specific situations to help children practice asking to be included in a game, waiting for a turn, playing with a different friend, or finding something different to do.

DO   the "Can I Play?" activity sheet. Children draw pictures showing how they might feel if they were left out and what they might do to correct the situation.

RELATE   the theme of the story you read to what goes on in the classroom and at school. Have the children show their drawings and share stories about times they wanted to join a game. Encourage students to use kind words and choose to include all children on a regular basis.

How to Be an Ambassador of Peace

LEARNING OBJECTIVES

Students will:

- explore what an Ambassador of Peace is and does
- learn specific skills they can use to become Ambassadors of Peace

MATERIALS NEEDED

The book *The Peace Book* by Todd Parr, "How to Be an Ambassador of Peace" activity sheet (page 35), writing and drawing tools, and poster board

LESSON PLAN

READ *The Peace Book*. This is a description of the many ways students can choose to promote peace.

> An optional text for teacher shared reading is *Peace Begins with Me* edited by Jill Bennett. The book, an anthology of poems about conflict, starts in the playground and moves outward from the personal to the global, taking in ownership, rights, respect, justice, and peace.

DISCUSS situations in the classroom, on the playground, at home, and in the community where students can use their skills to respect and support one another.

DO the "How to Be an Ambassador of Peace" activity sheet. Students record the things they can say and do, and how they feel. Connect their actions to how Ambassadors of Peace treat other people.

RELATE how being Ambassadors of Peace should become a regular part of life at school. Explain how the program at school will work and how students will be recognized for being Ambassadors of Peace (page 8). Have students share what they think they can do to become ambassadors. Read a poem from *Peace Begins with Me* (see above) to encourage students to take ownership on issues of respect, justice, and empathy.

Me and My Safe & Caring School Quiz

Use the quiz activity sheet (page 36) to review and assess what the students learned this month. *(Answers: 1-T, 2-F, 3-T, 4-F, 5-T, 6-Promise, 7-left, 8-care, 9-one)*

SAFE & CARING VOCABULARY BUILDER

Word Find

O	P	L	E	H	D	E	O	O
A	R	X	Q	O	F	I	C	C
P	O	E	Y	A	U	Z	A	A
E	M	O	S	E	L	U	R	R
K	I	N	D	P	X	O	I	I
C	S	J	O	G	E	A	N	N
P	E	A	C	E	V	C	G	G
Y	L	I	M	A	F	L	T	T
U	O	S	C	H	O	O	L	L

Circle these words in the Word Find puzzle.
(Hint: Words can run up, down, forward, backward, or diagonally.)

Key Words:

SAFE

RULES

KIND

HELP

PEACE

Challenge Words:

PROMISE

FAMILY

RESPECT

CARING

SCHOOL

Fill in the blanks to spell the words.

_a_e   p__m_s_   r_l_s

c_r_n_   _i_d   h_l_

we are
a safe
& caring
SCHOOL.

SAFE & CARING PROMISE

We promise to ourselves and everyone here to do our best to follow the rules, be respectful, and make

a Safe & Caring School.

Student Signatures

_____   _____

_____   _____

_____   _____

_____   _____

_____   _____

_____   _____

_____   _____

_____

Teacher(s)

SAFE & CARING RULES

✔ Treat others with kindness.

✔ Ask for help.

✔ Be a good listener.

✔ Take turns.

✔ Be helpful.

✔ Share your feelings in a caring way.

✔ Keep your hands and feet to yourself.

✔ Have fun!

we are a safe & caring school.

GOLDEN RULE

Treat others the way you want to be treated...

...with respect!

we aRe a SaFe & CaRiNG SCHOOL.

THE GOLDEN RULE

I was kind to someone.

Someone was kind to me.

we aRe a safe & CARiNG SCHOOL.

GETTING TO KNOW YOU

Likes to read

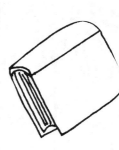

Likes music

Likes to draw

Has a brother

Plays sports

Loves mac & cheese

Likes to skate

Has a pet

Likes to swim

Has sisters

Rides a bike

Likes vegetables

THERE'S ONLY ONE OF ME!

Discover your name

My name is:

My name means:

_____

_____

_____

_____

_____

we are
a safe
& caring
school.

SEPTEMBER

Favorite things to do with my family are...

Family Facts

In my family, we have _____ people.

We have _____ grown-ups and _____ kids, and we have _____ pets.

My birthday is _____.

I was born...

in the town of _____,

in the state of _____, in the

country of _____.

What I like best about my family is...

My Family Book

Family Portrait

we are a safe & caring school.

Can I Play?

Have you ever been left out of the play group? Draw a picture to show how you felt and what you did.

HOW TO BE an
AMBASSADOR OF PEACE

Things I can say

_____
_____
_____
_____

Things I feel

_____
_____
_____
_____

Things I can do

_____
_____
_____
_____
_____

WE ARE
A SAFE
& CARING
SCHOOL.

Me and My Safe & Caring School Quiz

True or False (circle the correct answer)

1) School is fun when I know the kids in my class. .... **True / False**

2) Rules do not help us get along. .... **True / False**

3) The golden rule is about respecting others. .... **True / False**

4) Caring is not important at school. .... **True / False**

5) We can all be Ambassadors of Peace. .... **True / False**

Fill in the Blanks

Use the following words to complete each sentence:

left   one   care   promise

6) We made a Safe & Caring _____ together.

7) No one deserves to be _____ out.

8) When we _____ about each other, school is fun.

9) There is only _____ of me.

Draw or Write

10) How are you a safe and caring student?

we are
a safe
& caring
school.

SKILLS FOR SCHOOL. SKILLS FOR LIFE.

OCTOBER
Discovering Our Feelings

- **Awareness and Appropriate Expression of Feelings**
- **Anger Management**

- **Problem Solving**
- **Assertiveness**

Empathy and the ability to communicate effectively are key qualities children need in order to get along with others. Before we teach them to be assertive, children should recognize the causes and effects of negative attitudes and behaviors. They need to realize they have the power to choose how to respond to conflict. Being "emotionally fit" helps children face daily challenges in positive ways.

MONTHLY OBJECTIVES
Students will:

- learn to identify and express their feelings appropriately through role-play and other activities
- learn two strategies: "Stop, Think, Choose" and "I-messages" to help them resolve conflict in a positive way

TEACHING TIPS

- Provide children with a sense of belonging.
- Get to know your students.
- Build trusting relationships.
- Give students an opportunity to share something about themselves.

OCTOBER INTEGRATED ACTIVITIES

In addition to the specific lesson plans for this month, you can use these optional ideas to integrate and extend the Safe & Caring themes into daily routines and across the curricular areas.

LANGUAGE ARTS

- Play charades to familiarize students with key feelings words, such as *mad, sad, scared,* and *happy*. Let students pick feelings words from a bag or box, and act them out. After the class guesses the feeling, ask them to share personal experiences with the feeling by finishing this sentence: I feel _____ when _____.

- Ask older students to visit the primary grades and read picture books on feelings to small groups of kids.

LITERATURE

- Create book review clubs. Once a week encourage students to give their expert opinions on the books they read, focusing on the feelings of the characters.

- Students can create a classroom picture book of short stories regarding feelings.

- Read *Word Wizard* by Cathryn Falwell. Through Annie's adventures, the students will learn about anagrams. Use magnetic letters on a board that can be arranged to show the different anagrams from the story. Provide students with letters that spell one word, and ask them to spell another word using the same letters.

- Divide the class into small groups. Give each group three or four letters of the alphabet. Ask the students to come up with as many feelings words as they can that start with those letters. When they complete their list, have all groups work together to create a feelings dictionary.

SOCIAL STUDIES

- Students decorate a school bulletin board using words and pictures to describe different feelings.

ART

- Have students create posters for the classroom that each focus on one feelings word. As new feelings words are learned, add to the poster collection. Try different shapes for the posters.

- Each student can create a self-portrait showing specific feelings, such as happy, mad, sad, or scared. Use the portraits to talk about appropriate ways to express those feelings.

MUSIC

- Listen to the songs about feelings on the CDs *Ideas, Thoughts, and Feelings* and *Getting to Know Myself* by Hap Palmer (www.happalmer.com). Discuss the lyrics or do the related activities listed at the website.

MATH

- Students keep a tally of the feelings they see expressed in their classroom for a week, and then they create pictographs or bar graphs of the results. During circle time, discuss how many feelings they saw expressed and in what types of situations.

- Use *Monster Musical Chairs (MathStart 1)* by Stuart J. Murphy to learn math facts.

Safe & Caring Schools Vocabulary Builder

LEARNING OBJECTIVES

Students will:

- be introduced to vocabulary that supports learning how to express their feelings and understanding how feelings relate to a safe and caring classroom
- internalize the vocabulary as they use it throughout the month and year in real-life situations

MATERIALS NEEDED

Pencils and "Safe & Caring Vocabulary Builder" activity sheet (page 44)

LESSON PLAN

Use the vocabulary activities to introduce the concepts and common language of this month's theme. Throughout the month, use the words in writing, spelling, storytelling, and dealing with conflict situations. Add the words to your word wall.

For the Word Find activity, choose to use the key words, challenge words, or both. Discuss what the words mean after completing the page. You may want students to work in pairs to help each other complete the word find puzzle.

For the fill-in-the-blanks activity at the bottom of the page, students use vowels to fill in the missing letters to complete the words (*sad, happy, feelings, scared, strong, mad*).

Feelings Soup

LEARNING OBJECTIVES

Students will:

- learn to identify how they feel in different situations
- practice using words to express their feelings

MATERIALS NEEDED

The book *Smile-A-Saurus!* by Matt Mitter, "Feelings Soup" activity sheet (page 45), and pencils or pens

LESSON PLAN

READ *Smile-A-Saurus!* In this fun book, the dinosaurs love to express their feelings.

> An optional text for teacher shared reading is *Today I Feel Silly & Other Moods That Make My Day* by Jamie Lee Curtis. The story follows a little girl with curly red hair through 13 different moods.

DISCUSS how we all have different kinds of feelings. Feelings can make us comfortable or uncomfortable, especially when we feel mad, sad, scared, or embarrassed. Explain to students that all our feelings are important, but sometimes we are not sure how to use the right words to share how we feel. When our feelings get mixed up, it may be hard to say the right thing. If we learn to share our feelings in a caring way, we get along better with our friends.

DO the "Feelings Soup" activity sheet. Have children unscramble the words: sorry, silly, happy, proud, glad, shy, loved, sad, hurt, scared, mad, upset.

RELATE to the children how important it is to be able to identify how we are feeling and to express ourselves in an appropriate manner. Talk about how friends care about how their friends are feeling, too. That is one thing friends do.

Feelings Musical Chairs

LEARNING OBJECTIVES

Students will:

- learn to identify different feelings
- practice appropriate expressions of feelings

MATERIALS NEEDED

The book *The Way I Feel* by Janan Cain, "Feelings Musical Chairs" activity sheets (pages 46–47, there are two versions, one with words and one with faces), a chair for each participant, CD player, and music CD

LESSON PLAN

READ *The Way I Feel*. From scared to shy and bored to jealous, Cain covers the full spectrum of emotions in a series of rhymes and drawings. This book gives children the vocabulary they need to understand and express how they feel.

An optional book for teacher shared reading is *The Hating Book* by Charlotte Zolotow. When a girl's friend ignores her completely, bad feelings get out of hand.

DISCUSS what feelings the children think they use the most. Are they happy more than sad, silly more than serious? What are the most common feelings they feel? Help the kids name all the feelings presented in the book.

DO the "Feelings Musical Chairs" activity. Cut apart one set of the feelings cards from both sheets (words and faces). Set up a row of chairs (one chair per child) and label each chair with a feeling word and/or face, depending on your students' reading abilities. Have students march around the chairs while the music is playing. Instruct them that when the music stops, they sit on a chair. Ask each student to look at the feeling on the chair and to complete one of the following sentences using their feeling word (practicing past, present, and future tenses). Also, ask the students to demonstrate the feelings with their facial expressions.

- I felt excited when... *(I got a bike for my birthday)*.
- I feel happy because... *(my friend plays with me)*.
- I will feel sad if... *(someone pushes me)*.

RELATE the activity to daily life in the classroom. Tell the children that throughout the year you will help them practice using their words to express their feelings. You want to help them get along with others.

I Feel

LEARNING OBJECTIVES

Students will:

- identify how they feel in different situations
- learn the importance of sharing their feelings in positive ways

MATERIALS NEEDED

The book *Matthew and Tilly* by Rebecca C. Jones, "I Feel..." activity sheet (page 48), and pencils or pens

LESSON PLAN

READ *Matthew and Tilly*. Even the best of friends occasionally get on each other's nerves. In this story, a cool-down period is needed to think through things, and before too long, the friends are back together.

An optional text for teacher shared reading is *Let's Be Enemies* by Janice May Udry. James and John are best friends. When James always wants to be the boss, John doesn't want to be his friend anymore. But when John goes to James' house to tell him so, something unexpected happens.

DISCUSS Explain to students that we have different feelings depending upon what happens to us. *(I feel happy when a friend wants to play with me. I feel sad when I get pushed around)*. Ask students to think about things that have recently happened to them. How did they feel?

DO the "I Feel..." activity sheet. For nonreaders, read the questions aloud and ask them to color in the appropriate feelings face. You could make a transparency of the sheet and do it with the group on the overhead projector.

RELATE the activity sheet to daily life by comparing the similarities and differences in how students responded to the given situations. Explain that not everyone reacts the same way or feels the same emotions in a similar situation.

Bugs in a Row

LEARNING OBJECTIVES

Students will:

- learn that negative feelings are normal
- discover how to match feelings with their reactions to different situations

MATERIALS NEEDED

The book *The Grouchy Ladybug* by Eric Carle, "Bugs in a Row" activity sheet (page 49), and scissors

LESSON PLAN

READ *The Grouchy Ladybug*. A grouchy ladybug challenges everyone she meets. After a series of events, the bad-tempered ladybug becomes a happier, better-behaved bug.

> An optional text for teacher shared reading is *I'm Frustrated* by Elizabeth Crary. This is a story with many endings, which makes for interesting reading and teaches kids multiple ways to handle their own frustrations.

DISCUSS how students can share their feelings with words, as well as expressions. Help kids connect a positive attitude to feelings of happiness as opposed to feelings of grouchiness and stubbornness.

DO the "Bugs in a Row" activity sheet. Have students cut out the nine bugs on the sheet. There are three happy, three mad, and three sad bugs to choose from in this game. One at a time, read aloud the statements below. Have students place the bug that shows how they would feel on the corresponding numbered space on the activity sheet. When all the statements have been read, each child should have three of the same bugs in a row, either up, down, or diagonally.

Statements:

1) You are invited to a birthday party. 2) Your kitten is lost. 3) You get pushed at recess. 4) Someone breaks your favorite toy. 5) You get a new pet. 6) It's raining and you cannot go outside to play. 7) The other kids don't want to play with you. 8) Someone cuts in front of you in line. 9) You get a new bike.

RELATE what the children have learned about their feelings to how they can respond to school situations. Discuss the different answers to some of the statements. Why were some mad and others sad about an event? Remind the children that it is important to know what to do with their feelings.

Catch That Feeling

LEARNING OBJECTIVES

Students will:

- review and match common emotions with facial expressions
- learn appropriate emotional responses to different situations

MATERIALS NEEDED

The book *Glad Monster, Sad Monster* by Ed Emberley and Anne Miranda, "Catch That Feeling" activity sheet (page 50), and pencils or pens

LESSON PLAN

READ *Glad Monster, Sad Monster*. Friendly monsters talk about specific feelings, enabling children and adults to discuss their emotions in an easy and nonthreatening way.

> An optional text for teacher shared reading is *When You're Shy and You Know It* by Elizabeth Crary and Shari Steelsmith. This book helps young children learn how to express feelings in healthy ways.

DISCUSS the various emotions in the story. Help children relate their feelings to their own experiences.

DO the "Catch That Feeling" activity sheet. Children complete the three sections.

Section 1: Fill in the missing letter to complete the word. Then match the word to the fish's expression by drawing a line between the fishing rod and the fish.

Section 2: Count the number of fish with matching expressions and write that number in the box provided *(happy 5, sad 4, mad 3, scared 3)*.

Section 3: Draw in the fish face and/or write the feeling (from the four feelings in Sections 1 and 2) to complete the sentences *(mad, scared, happy)*.

RELATE to the children how important it is to match how they feel inside with how they look outside. This will better enable them to express how they feel and help them begin to recognize the feelings of others by reading their body language.

What Happens When I Get Angry?

LEARNING OBJECTIVES

Students will:

- gain a better understanding of what happens to their bodies when they feel angry
- learn positive ways to transition from anger to calmness

MATERIALS NEEDED

The book *When I Feel Angry* by Cornelia Maude Spelman, "What Happens When I Get Angry?" activity sheet (page 51), and pencils or pens

LESSON PLAN

READ   *When I Feel Angry*. A little rabbit describes what makes her angry and how she can control her anger.

An optional text for teacher shared reading is *When You're Mad and You Know It* by Elizabeth Crary and Shari Steelsmith. Designed to help kids learn to talk about emotions, the rhymes advise angry kids to "blow air out," "shake it out," and "give a shout."

DISCUSS   Remind students that expressing their feelings is important, but it is never okay to hurt others when they are angry. Brainstorm negative choices people make to express their anger *(yell, throw things, hit)* and better ways to express feelings.

DO   the "What Happens When I Get Angry?" activity sheet. Make a transparency for the overhead projector to help lead the students through their own sheets. Use the picture and descriptions in 1 to talk about how the children may feel when they get angry. As the calming techniques in 2 are read, have children circle the ones they use to help them get to 3, all calmed down.

RELATE   the consequences of expressing anger in a negative way to what the children can do in school to appropriately express their anger. In circle time, have children share their favorite choices for calming down when they are angry.

Stop, Think, Choose

LEARNING OBJECTIVES

Students will:

- learn the simple three-step process of Stop, Think, Choose
- practice the process to help them remain calm and resolve conflicts in a positive way

MATERIALS NEEDED

The book *Franklin's Bad Day* by Paulette Bourgeois, one copy of a pre-colored "Stop, Think, Choose" miniposter (page 52)

LESSON PLAN

READ   *Franklin's Bad Day*. When Franklin has a bad day, he takes out his anger on others. His father teaches him how to make a better choice and find a way to share his feelings without hurting anyone.

An optional text for teacher shared reading is *The Quarreling Book* by Charlotte Zolotow. Gruffness and anger is passed along from person to person until a little dog starts a chain of happiness that reverses the trend.

DISCUSS   how Franklin behaved when he was angry. How was that negative and destructive behavior? What was the better choice that he learned from his father?

DO   Show the children the "Stop, Think, Choose" miniposter you prepared before this activity. Talk about a real stoplight and what the colors stand for. Explain that in the classroom, the red stands for "Stop," yellow for "Think," and green for "Choose." Explain that Stop, Think, Choose is one of the ways we will use to solve problems. Teach these three steps for staying calm when angry or dealing with conflict:

1. Stop: Slow down. Breathe deeply. Relax.
2. Think: What's the problem? How am I feeling? How is the other person feeling? What options do I have for solving the problem?
3. Choose: Use safe and caring words to make a good choice.

Practice Stop, Think, Choose by role-playing these situations: taking turns, not sharing, being laughed at in a game, cheating on assignments, cutting in line. Add your own situations, too.

RELATE to the class that sometimes, no matter how hard they try to make the right choice, they cannot solve problems by themselves. Remind them that they can always ask an adult for help.

I-Message

LEARNING OBJECTIVES

Students will:

- learn about I-messages
- practice I-messages by positively expressing how they feel during conflicts

MATERIALS NEEDED

The book *Ruby the Copycat* by Peggy Rathmann, "I-Message" activity sheet (page 53), and pencils or pens

LESSON PLAN

READ *Ruby the Copycat.* Ruby insists on copying Angela until her teacher helps her discover her own creative talents.

An optional text for teacher shared reading is *I'm Mad* by Elizabeth Crary. It guides children to consider various healthy ways of expressing and letting go of angry feelings.

DISCUSS Ask children to identify all the feelings Angela and Ruby have during the story. Discuss that even best friends can hurt each other's feelings with what they say or do. Explore better ways to express feelings when upset with a friend or when there is a problem.

DO the "I-Message" activity sheet. Go back to the story. Read the note that Angela wrote to Ruby. Ask the children how they could change the note using an I-message. For nonwriters, make an overhead transparency of the sheet and write it together as a class.

RELATE that it may take students time to remember how to use I-messages, but they will have plenty of opportunities to practice. Refer to I-messages often, especially during teachable moments. As you read books dealing with conflict, encourage the students to suggest how the characters in the stories could use I-messages to resolve their conflicts.

Safe & Caring Hearts

LEARNING OBJECTIVES

Students will:

- learn how to use words to express their feelings
- use I-messages to help them express their feelings in positive ways during conflicts

MATERIALS NEEDED

The book *I Can't Wait* by Elizabeth Crary, laminated copies of "Safe & Caring Hearts" activity sheet (page 54)

LESSON PLAN

READ *I Can't Wait.* This book describes real-life situations where patience is needed. It helps children identify alternative solutions to common daily problems.

An optional text for teacher shared reading is *Let's Be Patient* by P. K. Hallinan.

DISCUSS specific things students can do in the classroom, on the playground, and in other areas of school when they get into arguments with friends. Review I-message steps.

DO the "Safe & Caring Hearts" activity page. Have students cut out the two laminated hearts. Demonstrate how to use the two caring hearts in conjunction with I-messages to resolve conflict in a peaceful way. Use this example or one of your own.

1. Tou wants to play with Jamie and the toy she has. Jamie pushes Tou and tells him she doesn't want to play with him. Tou's feelings are hurt, but he knows he needs to use the right words to resolve the conflict. Tou takes the heart with the bandage, shows it to Jamie, and uses an I-message to say, "I feel hurt when you push me, and I need you to share with me."

2. Tou and Jamie are playing well together and sharing toys. Tou shows the smiling heart to Jamie and tells her he feels happy when she shares with him.

RELATE the "Safe and Caring Hearts" examples to situations the students have in your classroom or on the playground. Have the kids practice using I-messages along with the hearts.

Discovering Our Feelings Quiz

Use the quiz activity sheet (page 55) to review and assess what the students learned this month. *(Answers: 1-T, 2-T, 3-T, 4-T, 5-F, 6-Stop, Think, Choose, 7-messages)*

SAFE & CARING
VOCABULARY BUILDER

Word Find

S	P	L	U	P	S	E	T
U	H	X	E	O	M	I	C
R	O	Y	P	P	A	H	A
P	R	O	U	D	D	U	G
R	I	N	P	R	X	O	N
I	S	J	S	A	D	A	I
S	O	A	E	E	V	Z	V
E	X	C	I	T	E	D	O
D	A	L	G	H	A	O	L

Circle these words in the Word Find puzzle.

(Hint: Words can run up, down, forward, backward, or diagonally.)

Key Words:
GLAD

SAD

MAD

SHY

HAPPY

Challenge Words:
SURPRISED

EXCITED

UPSET

LOVING

PROUD

Fill in the blanks with vowels to complete the words.

s _ d   f _ _ l _ ngs   str _ ng

h _ ppy   sc _ r _ d   m _ d

FEELINGS SOUP

Unscramble the mixed-up feelings words.

Sometimes our feelings are all mixed up.

spte u

yaph

racdes

rgda

list yl

urpp

esp

roy sr

turh

hys

and

ovla

Write the words on the lines below.

WE ARE
A SAFE
& CARING
SCHOOL.

OCTOBER

FEELINGS MUSICAL CHAIRS

 **Happy**

 **Scared**

 **Sad**

 **Proud**

 **Angry**

 **Tired**

 **Silly**

 **Hurt**

 **Lonely**

 **Sorry**

 **Excited**

 **Loved**

 Add your own feeling

 Add your own feeling

 Add your own feeling

we are
a safe
& caring
school.

FEELINGS MUSICAL CHAIRS

 Silly

 Hurt

 Lonely

 Sorry

 Excited

 Loved

we are
a safe
& caring
school.

I FeeL ...

OCTOBER

Color the face that shows how you might feel if...

Happy	Sad	Mad	Scared	
				...someone says, "I don't like you."
				...someone takes your things without asking.
				...you get to ride your bike.
				...you're blamed for something you didn't do.
				...you get to play with your friends.
				...a bully pushes you around.
				...you get invited to a birthday party.
				...someone makes fun of you.
				...a friend helps you.
				...someone yells at you.
				...you win a game.
				...you forget your homework at home.
				...someone gives you a gift.

we are a safe & caring school.

BUGS IN A ROW

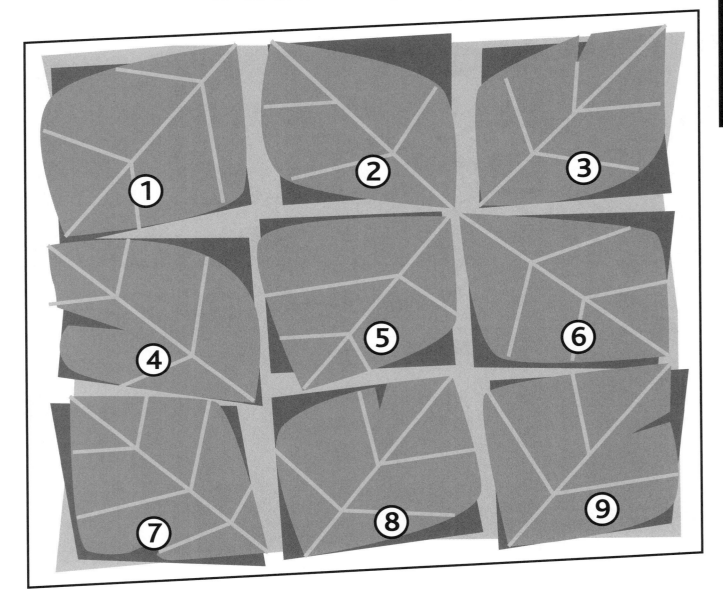

From *Activities for Building Character and Social-Emotional Learning Grades 1–2* by Katia S. Petersen, Ph.D., copyright © 2012. Free Spirit Publishing Inc., Minneapolis, MN; 800-735-7323; www.freespirit.com.
This page may be reproduced for individual, classroom, and small group work only. For all other uses, contact www.freespirit.com/company/permissions.cfm.

CATCH THAT FEELING

h__ppy
sa__
__ad
scar__d

Complete each word and match it to the fish.

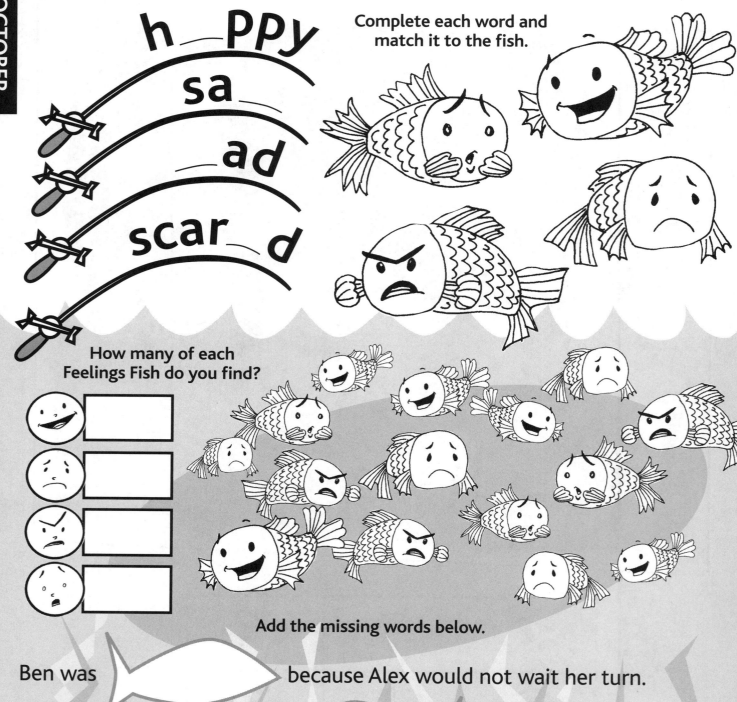

How many of each Feelings Fish do you find?

Add the missing words below.

Ben was _____ because Alex would not wait her turn.

Lucy was _____ of the bully.

Oliver was _____ when he won the game!

WE ARE a SAFE & CARiNG SCHOOL.

OCTOBER

WHAT HAPPENS WHEN I GET

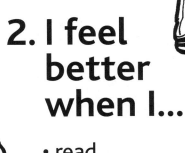

ANGRY?

1. When I get angry...

- my heart races.
- my face feels hot.
- my eyes hurt.
- my muscles get tight.
- I get sweaty.
- my hands turn into fists.
- I get a headache.
- my stomach hurts.

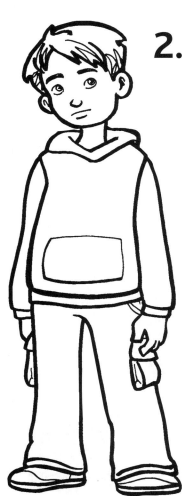

2. I feel better when I...

- read.
- exercise.
- draw.
- listen to music.
- talk to a friend.
- breathe deeply.
- talk to a grown-up.
- count to 10.
- have quiet time.
- take a walk.

3. Now I'm calm.

We aRe a SaFe & CaRiNG SCHOOL.

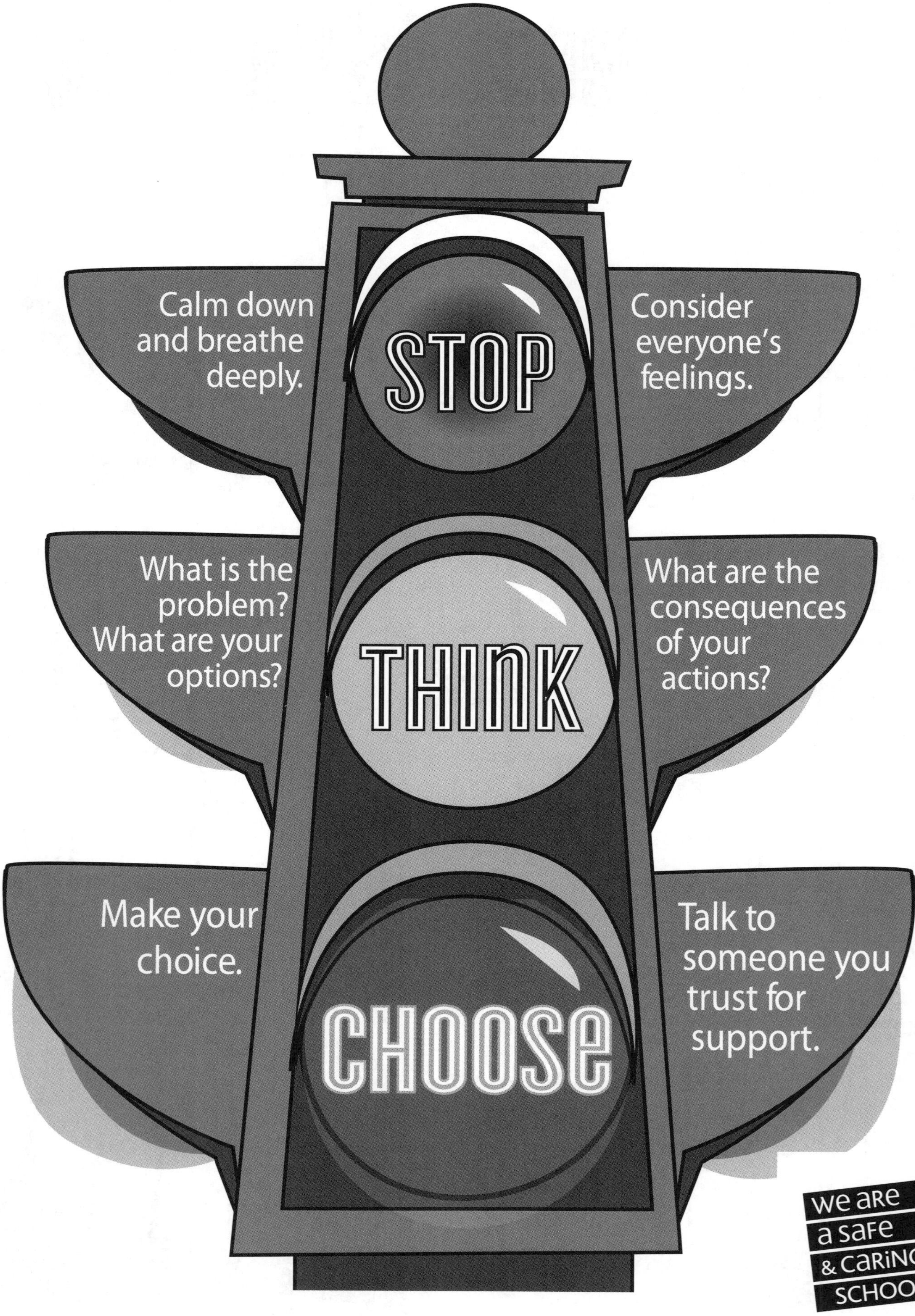

Calm down and breathe deeply.

Consider everyone's feelings.

STOP

What is the problem? What are your options?

What are the consequences of your actions?

THINK

Make your choice.

Talk to someone you trust for support.

CHOOSE

we are a safe & caring SCHOOL.

I-Message

I feel... (write how you feel)

Happy   Sad   Mad   Scared

_____

_____

_____

_____

when you... (write what happened)

_____

_____

_____

_____

I need... (write what you need to make things better)

_____

_____

_____

_____

we aRe
a saFe
& CaRiNG
SCHOOL.

safe & caring hearts

we are
a safe
& caring
school.

DISCOVERING OUR FEELINGS QUIZ

True or False (circle the correct answer)

1) It is good to say what you feel. ....**True / False**

2) My feelings can get all mixed up. ....**True / False**

3) Feelings are very important. ....**True / False**

4) I can calm down when I get angry. ....**True / False**

5) Other people's feelings are not important. ....**True / False**

Fill in the Blanks

Fill in the blanks to complete each sentence.

6) We can s__ __ __, t__ __ __ __, c__ __ __ __ __
to make good decisions when we are angry.

7) We say how we feel when we use I-__ __ __ __ __ __ __ __.

Draw or Write

8) How do you feel at school today?

"My role in the school is to work with the teachers and the curriculum in all areas, and integrate it with the state frameworks. The way the Safe & Caring Schools program is written, it flows very easily into all areas: social studies, writing, literacy."

TEACHER—FROST SCHOOL

SKILLS FOR SCHOOL. SKILLS FOR LIFE.

NOVEMBER
Caring People—My Support System

- **Creating a Support System**
- **Asking for Help**

- **Friendship**
- **Appreciation**

It is essential that adults recognize and take seriously the stress in our children's lives. Today, students worry about family issues, friends, academic performance, peer pressure, and much more. Adults should model healthy ways of dealing with stress and create a support system where children can practice asking for help appropriately.

MONTHLY OBJECTIVES
Students will:

- learn the importance of a support system and how to ask for help from people they know and trust
- discuss the qualities of friendship and how good friends can be an important part of their support system

TEACHING TIPS

- Model desirable behaviors. You set the tone for the kind of support system the children will trust.
- Use teachable moments to recognize and encourage acts of kindness and concern in your classroom and school.
- Integrate the teaching of social and emotional skills into every day.

NOVEMBER INTEGRATED ACTIVITIES

In addition to the specific lesson plans for this month, you can use these optional ideas to integrate and extend the Safe & Caring themes into daily routines and across the curricular areas.

LANGUAGE ARTS

- Have students draw a picture of a friend in class, interview him or her, and then introduce the friend to the rest of the class.

- Involve students in creating a list of the qualities of good friends. Post these qualities around the room as reminders of how to build positive friendships.

- Read *It's Time to Call 911: What to Do in an Emergency* by Julie Melie. Use a toy phone and have children practice dialing and asking for help during an emergency.

LITERATURE

- Read *Take Time to Relax!* by Nancy Carlson. The beavers in this tale represent the typical over-programmed family of today. After-school and after-work activities result in the family spending little time together—that is, until a major snowstorm arrives.

- Read *Jonathan James Says, "I Can Help"* by Crystal Bowman. Jonathan learns different ways he can be a good helper. Have students write a story about a time they asked for help from someone they know and trust.

- Read *How About a Hug?* by Nancy Carlson. Discover the many reasons a hug can be shared between two people who care about each other.

SOCIAL STUDIES

- Create a "Friendship Corner" on a bulletin board where students can post caring messages to each other.

- Have students bring photographs of their families or draw family portraits. As they introduce their family members to the class, have the kids talk about the kind of support they get from the members of their families.

ART

- Read *Degas and the Little Dancer* by Laurence Anholt. The little ballerina and the artist learn about empathy through their friendship. Students can draw or paint pictures about their friends and what they appreciate about them.

- Read either *Mama, Do You Love Me?* by Barbara M. Joose and Barbara Lavallee, or *Guess How Much I Love You* by Sam McBratney and Anita Jerom. Then have the children draw pictures to show how their families show love to each other.

- Create a classroom friendship collage or mural. Have students take turns adding their touches to the work of art until it is a finished masterpiece.

- Draw pictures showing how children can be good helpers at home and at school.

MUSIC

- Listen to songs from *Free to Be . . . You and Me* by Marlo Thomas and Friends (www.freetobefoundation.org). Many of the songs pertain to the themes of this month. Discuss the songs' messages with children.

MATH

- Read *Probably Pistachio* by Stuart J. Murphy. Jack is having a bad day. Students learn about probabilities as they watch Jack's day get better.

- Read *Caps for Sale: A Tale of a Peddler, Some Monkeys and Their Monkey Business* by Esphyr Slobodkina. Have fun with math problems using the story as a starting point.

Safe & Caring Schools Vocabulary Builder

LEARNING OBJECTIVES

Students will:

- be introduced to vocabulary related to support systems and learn that caring people are important in a safe and caring school
- internalize the vocabulary as they use it throughout the month and year in real-life situations

MATERIALS NEEDED

Pencils and "Safe & Caring Vocabulary Builder" activity sheet (page 64)

LESSON PLAN

Use the vocabulary activities to introduce the concepts and common language associated with this month's theme. Throughout the month, use the words in writing, spelling, storytelling, and when talking about caring people who support children. Add the words to your word wall.

For the Word Find activity, use the key words, challenge words, or both. Discuss what the words mean after completing the page. You may want students to work in pairs to help each other.

For the number code activity at the bottom of the page, have students solve the math problems to determine the vowels that complete the words: *ask, give, trust, words, stress, safe, home, caring, worry.*

People Who Care About Me

LEARNING OBJECTIVES

Students will:

- learn to identify a personal support system
- understand how to ask for help when they need it

MATERIALS NEEDED

The book *Spinky Sulks* by William Steig, "People Who Care About Me" activity sheet (page 65), pencils or pens, and colored pencils, markers, or crayons

LESSON PLAN

READ *Spinky Sulks*. This is a humorous, thoughtful exploration of a child's own private thoughts and feelings. Spinky is convinced that he is not loved by his family, until they show him that they do care.

> An optional text for teacher shared reading is *The Rag Coat* by Lauren Mills. A girl proudly wears her coat made of clothing scraps to school. The other children laugh at her until they hear the stories behind the scraps and learn about love, goodwill, and overcoming poverty.

DISCUSS Review the importance of having a support system, noting that everyone, even grown-ups, need to have people who care about them. Explain that the people who care about us can help us, especially when we are not sure what to do about a problem.

DO the "People Who Care About Me" activity sheet. Have the students draw up to eight faces of people who care about them at home, in the neighborhood, and at school. Include the names of the caring people.

RELATE the concept of a support system to how families, friends, and school staff are available when kids need someone to help. Remind children that you are one of the people who can help them by listening to their questions and problems and providing advice and helpful suggestions.

The Safe Thing to Do

LEARNING OBJECTIVES

Students will:

- identify situations where they need help
- learn how to ask for help when they need it in emergency situations

MATERIALS NEEDED

The book *I Can Be Safe* by Pat Thomas, "The Safe Thing to Do" activity sheet (page 66), and pencils or pens

LESSON PLAN

READ *I Can Be Safe*. This friendly book acknowledges children's fears and helps them become aware of things they need to do in order to feel safe in different situations.

An optional text for teacher shared reading is *The Class Trip* by Grace Maccarone. Sam has quite a scare when he gets separated from his group on a trip to the zoo. Sam learns an important lesson about protecting himself.

DISCUSS Review different situations where children need to ask for help. Differentiate between emergency and nonemergency situations.

DO "The Safe Thing to Do" activity sheet. Children draw a line to connect the problem with the appropriate helper. As a class, state the problem and then determine the best solution. Using the activity sheet as a guide, have children practice asking for help by choosing a situation from the sheet or another one of their own choosing.

RELATE the theme of the lesson to real-life situations in which kids may find themselves. Tell the children there are people who care about them and want them to be safe. It is smart to tell a trusted adult when something is wrong in order to get the help you need.

The Helper in Me

LEARNING OBJECTIVES

Students will:

- explore what it means to care
- learn the importance of helping others

MATERIALS NEEDED

The book *Amos & Boris* by William Steig, "The Helper in Me" activity sheet (page 67), and pencils or pens

LESSON PLAN

READ *Amos & Boris*. Befriended by a whale as he is drowning in the ocean, a mouse gets a chance to return the favor in an equally unlikely situation years later.

An optional text for teacher shared reading is *That's What Friends Are For* by Florence Parry Heide and Sylvia Van Clief. Theodore, an elephant, has hurt his leg. Stuck where he is, he ponders his plight and decides to ask his friends for advice because that's what friends are for.

DISCUSS how good friends help one another and how that was evident in the story you read. Emphasize that helping is part of getting along. Have children think of a time when they gave help to or received help from a good friend. Demonstrate specific things to say and do when someone needs help. For example, if someone looks upset, you might ask, "Are you okay? Can I help you?" or "Are you sad?" Acknowledge the children who reach out to others by thanking them for their helpfulness and kindness.

DO "The Helper in Me" activity sheet. On the top half, have children draw and/or write about a time when they were helpers. How did they help? How did the other person feel when getting help? How did the student feel after helping someone else? At the bottom of the page, complete the matching activity.

RELATE to the children that there is a helper inside all of us. In our safe and caring school, we help each other. Use the matching activity on the activity sheet to start a list of ways children can be good helpers at school and at home.

What Is a Friend?

LEARNING OBJECTIVES

Students will:

- identify the good qualities of a friendship
- practice their skills of getting along in small groups

MATERIALS NEEDED

The book *The Best Friends Book* by Todd Parr, "What Is a Friend?" activity sheet (page 68), magazines, poster board, pencils or pens, and markers or crayons

LESSON PLAN

READ *The Best Friends Book*. Friendship is shown to be unconditional and proven to be extremely important in this colorful book.

> An optional text for teacher shared reading is *Friends* by Helme Heine. Charlie Rooster, Johnny Mouse, and Percy the Pig are best friends, and they do everything together. When night falls, though, and it's time to go to bed, they learn that sometimes even friends have to be apart.

DISCUSS Review the qualities that are important in a friend. What do you look for in a friend? *(funny, good listener, shares, cares how you feel)* Ask children for examples of how to be a good friend and how to treat friends.

DO the "What Is a Friend?" activity sheet. Students are to draw a picture of a good friend and fill in the vowels to complete the words. Circle the thumbs-up or thumbs-down to indicate if the word names a good or bad quality of a friend.

Optional Friends Activity: Divide the class into small groups. Ask each group to create a poster using one of the following ideas: Things I like in a friend, things I like to do with friends, or ways friends help each other.

RELATE the idea of what makes a good friend to real-life situations. Ask students: Who do you know that qualifies as a good friend? What is it about that person that makes him or her a good friend? If posters are made, allow each group to take a turn presenting its poster to the rest of the class. Use the posters to decorate the hallway or create a bulletin board.

My Friend and I Can . . .

LEARNING OBJECTIVES

Students will:

- review what makes a good friend
- gain an understanding of how to make and keep friends

MATERIALS NEEDED

The book *We Are Best Friends* by Aliki, "My Friend and I Can…" activity sheet (page 69), pencils or pens, and crayons or markers

LESSON PLAN

READ *We Are Best Friends*. When his best friend Peter moves away, Robert has no one to play with, no one to fight with, and no fun at all. Then he meets Will and finds he's not the only one who needs a new best friend.

> An optional text for teacher shared reading is *George and Martha* by James Marshall. George and Martha, wise and funny hippos, teach each other the importance of honesty, companionship, discretion, humility, and consolation.

DISCUSS Explain to children that it is not always easy to be a friend, and even the best of friends have very hard days. Good friends help each other make things right. Note that sometimes friends move away. No matter how hard it is to lose a friend, children need to learn how to make new friends.

DO the "My Friend and I Can…" activity sheet. In acrostic fashion, have the children write things they can do with a friend that start with each of the letters in SHARE. Give an example, such as sit and talk, have a race, act silly, ride bikes, eat ice cream. Students can illustrate their phrases, too.

RELATE to the students how important it is to make and keep friends. Let them know that often we have to work at maintaining friends, and it is not always easy.

Share their responses on the activity sheets. Let the children know that even best friends forget how to get along sometimes. Encourage them to remind each other how to be good friends.

Friendship Rainbow

LEARNING OBJECTIVES

Students will:

- explore what it means to be unique
- learn to appreciate and accept the uniqueness of others

MATERIALS NEEDED

The book *A Rainbow of Friends* by P. K. Hallinan, "Friendship Rainbow" activity sheet (page 70), writing and coloring tools, scissors, butcher paper on which you prepare a large rainbow prior to class, box containing strips of paper with the students' names written on them

LESSON PLAN

READ *A Rainbow of Friends*. This book explains that each person is unique and adds immensely to the lives of others. Kids are encouraged to respect people who are disabled, to help those in trouble, and to reach out to the people around them.

> An optional text for teacher shared reading is *That's What a Friend Is* by P. K. Hallinan. This book is a celebration of the joys of childhood friendships told in lighthearted verse.

DISCUSS how friends come in all shapes and sizes, and with a variety of backgrounds and experiences. Friends also have different moods at times, and different ways of doing things. How do friends treat each other?

DO the "Friendship Rainbow" activity sheet. Have each child select one name from the name box and decorate either the girl or boy on the activity sheet to match the person whose name was drawn. After coloring the person, the child should cut it out by cutting around the outline. In the large group, have the children name who they drew, give that person a friendship compliment, and attach the cutout to the large rainbow you prepared so it holds hands with its neighbor.

RELATE what the class learned about being accepting of others to how they should treat one another in school. In circle time, gather children around the Friendship Rainbow and point out that even though everyone is unique and special, they all have a place in the classroom rainbow of friends.

Warm Thank You

LEARNING OBJECTIVES

Students will:

- learn about empathy and caring for others
- discover different ways people care for one another

MATERIALS NEEDED

The book *The Mitten Tree* by Candace Christiansen, "Warm and Caring" activity sheet (page 71), and writing and coloring tools

LESSON PLAN

READ *The Mitten Tree*. Old Sarah knits mittens for all the children waiting for the school bus, and she hangs them on the spruce tree at the bus stop. Though she has used all her yarn, Sarah returns home with a full heart and discovers a surprise waiting on her porch.

> An optional text for teacher shared reading is *My Best Friend* by Pat Hutchins. Two girls demonstrate that someone who can run fast, climb high, and read books is certainly special. But being able to comfort a frightened friend is equally important.

DISCUSS   how Sarah showed she cared about the children, even though she never talked to them. How can the class show others they care?

DO the "Warm and Caring" card activity. Have children draw or write a caring message in the cards for someone in their families, someone at school, or residents of an adult care facility. If making cards for adult care residents, plan a field trip to the care facility to distribute the cards.

RELATE the warm feelings children can create by being generous to how they can have those feelings in school, too. Talk about what others do for the students and name the specific things for which the children are grateful. Conclude with ways they can show they care for others at school.

Wonder About Worries

LEARNING OBJECTIVES

Students will:

- learn that worrying is normal
- understand that when they are worried, they can ask for help from people they know and trust

MATERIALS NEEDED

The book *Wemberly Worried* by Kevin Henkes, "Wonder About Worries" activity sheet (page 72), and pencils or pens

LESSON PLAN

READ *Wemberly Worried.* Wemberly the Mouse worries about everything, big things and small things, until her teacher introduces her to a new friend.

An optional text for teacher shared reading is *Silly Billy* by Anthony Browne. A young boy worries so much that his grandmother gives him Guatemalan worry dolls. Then, he worries he is overwhelming the dolls.

DISCUSS what it feels like to worry. Why do we worry? What can we do when we start to worry? Who can we go to for help?

DO the "Wonder About Worries" activity sheet. Have students record their answers to worrying prompts. This activity may be done as a whole-class activity on a transparency and overhead projector.

RELATE excessive worrying to being counterproductive. There are some things people, especially children, have no control over, so it does no good to worry. When they start to worry, children should find a person they trust to talk about what is bothering them.

Good Helpers

LEARNING OBJECTIVES

Students will:

- learn how to solve problems in peaceful ways
- explore ways they can be positive bystanders

MATERIALS NEEDED

The book *The Lion and the Mouse* by Aesop and retold by Gail Herman, "Good Helpers" activity sheet (page 73), pencils or pens, and markers or crayons

LESSON PLAN

READ *The Lion and the Mouse,* which is a retelling of an Aesop's fable. A powerful lion catches a mouse that begs the beast to free him. In return, the mouse says he will help the lion someday. Amused, the lion frees the mouse.

An optional text for teacher shared reading is *Edwina, the Dinosaur Who Didn't Know She Was Extinct* by Mo Willems. Everyone loves Edwina, except the class know-it-all Reginald Von Hoobie-Doobie who tries to convince everyone that dinosaurs are extinct.

DISCUSS Review the story. Why did the lion let the mouse go? How was the small mouse brave enough to help the lion when he was in trouble? Did the mouse do what he promised?

DO the "Good Helpers" activity sheet. Discuss how students can help in small ways when they notice that a friend might be in trouble. Have the students draw or write what they would do in each situation. For class discussion, do this activity with an overhead transparency.

RELATE how friends can support each other to do the right thing. Discuss what a bystander is (someone who sees another child being hurt) and encourage students to be positive bystanders (stepping in to help when possible, or getting others to help).

Caring People— My Support System Quiz

Use the quiz activity sheet (page 74) to review and assess what the students learned this month. *(Answers: 1-T, 2-F, 3-F, 4-T, 5-T, 6-help, 7-talk, 8-school, home, 9-teacher)*

Safe & Caring
Vocabulary Builder

Word Find

S	S	E	R	T	S	P	A
U	U	X	K	O	D	I	J
R	A	P	P	Z	N	O	G
P	E	O	P	L	E	U	N
H	I	N	P	O	I	O	I
O	S	T	S	U	R	T	R
M	O	A	A	E	F	T	A
E	Q	I	F	O	D	S	C
G	I	V	E	H	K	O	M

Circle these words in the Word Find puzzle.
(Hint: Words can run up, down, forward, backward, or diagonally.)

Key Words:
ASK

GIVE

HOME

SAFE

TRUST

Challenge Words:
CARING

FRIENDS

STRESS

SUPPORT

PEOPLE

Solve the math problems. Use the number code to finish the words.

Number Code: 1=a   2=e   3=i   4=o   5=u

3 − 2 = __ = __sk   2 + 2 = __ = w__rds   1 + 3 = __ = h__me

2 + 1 = __ = g__ve   4 − 2 = __ = str__ss   4 − 3 = __ = c__ring

2 + 3 = __ = tr__st   5 − 4 = __ = s__fe   3 + 1 = __ = w__rry

we are
a safe
& caring
school.

PEOPLE WHO CARE ABOUT ME

At School

At Home and in My Neighborhood

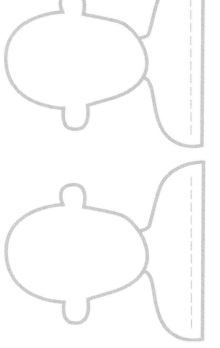

From *Activities for Building Character and Social-Emotional Learning Grades 1–2* by Katia S. Petersen, Ph.D., copyright © 2012. Free Spirit Publishing Inc., Minneapolis, MN; 800-735-7323; www.freespirit.com.

THE SAFE THING TO DO

Match the problem with the helper.

Problem   Solution

we aRe
a SaFe
& CaRiNG
SCHOOL.

THE HELPER IN ME

Draw or write a story about a time you helped a friend.

NOVEMBER

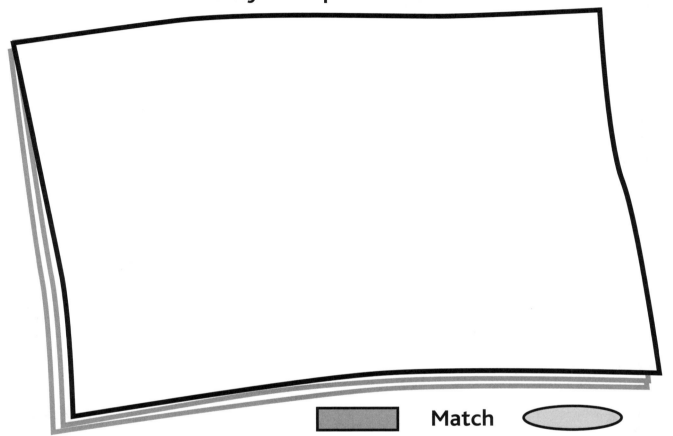

Match

If a friend falls down,

If a friend is using unkind words,

If a friend is sad,

If a friend looks lonely,

If a friend forgot his or her markers,

I'll make my friend laugh.

I'll play with my friend.

I'll help my friend up.

I'll ask my friend to stop.

I'll share mine.

we are a safe & caring school.

 # WHAT IS A FRIEND?

Draw a picture of someone being a good friend.

Use vowels to complete words that might describe a friend.
Circle thumbs-up if it's good or thumbs-down if it's bad.

a   e   i   o   u

Sh☐res  or

H☐lps  or

B☐ssy  or

H☐ts 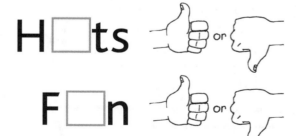 or

F☐n 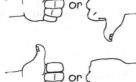 or

 we aRe
a saFe
& CaRiNG
SCHOOL.

MY FRIEND AND I CAN...

**S
H
A
R
E**

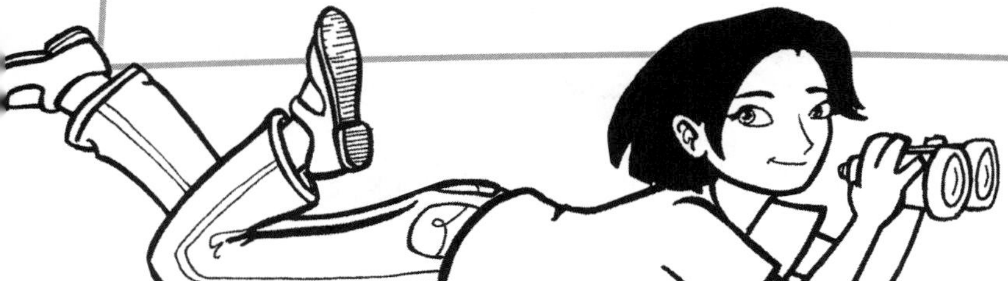

_____
_____
_____
_____
_____
_____
_____
_____
_____
_____
_____
_____
_____
_____
_____
_____
_____
_____
_____

WE ARE
A SAFE
& CARiNG
SCHOOL.

FRIENDSHIP RAINBOW

WE ARE A SAFE & CARING SCHOOL.

Warm and Caring

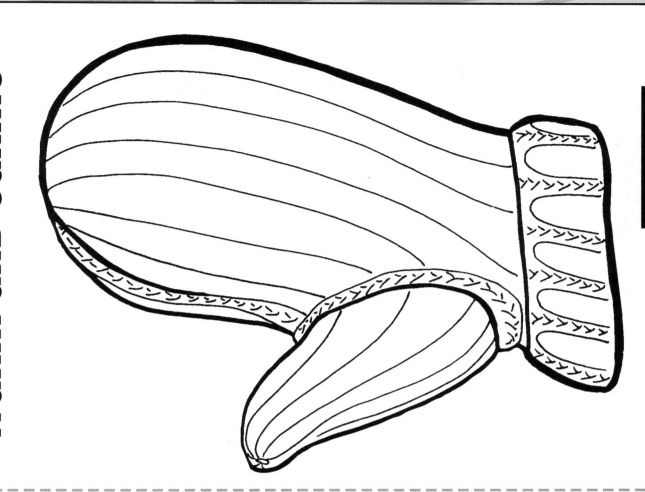

We are a safe & caring school.

NOVEMBER

WONDER ABOUT WORRIES

Some things I worry about are...

_____

_____

_____

_____

_____

_____

Something I can do to feel better when I worry is...

_____

_____

_____

_____

_____

_____

People I can talk to about my worries are...

_____

_____

_____

_____

_____

When someone comes to me with a worry, I...

_____

_____

_____

_____

_____

we are a safe & caring school.

When friends need us we can all be...

GOOD HELPERS

Draw or write what you would do in each of these situations

The girls are whispering with each other and pointing at another girl.

Izabelle does not want Maria to play with Jessie anymore.

Adam tells Michael he needs his help to take away the ball from José.

Two boys are laughing and pointing at another boy.

we aRe a saFe & CaRiNG SCHOOL.

From *Activities for Building Character and Social-Emotional Learning Grades 1–2* by Katia S. Petersen, Ph.D., copyright © 2012. Free Spirit Publishing Inc., Minneapolis, MN; 800-735-7323; www.freespirit.com.

CARING PEOPLE—MY SUPPORT SYSTEM QUIZ

True or False (circle the correct answer)

1) Sometimes we all need help. .... **True / False**

2) Only wimps worry. .... **True / False**

3) Needing help is a sign of weakness. .... **True / False**

4) I know there are people who care about me. .... **True / False**

5) I can get help from others at my safe and
caring school. .... **True / False**

Fill in the Blanks

Use these words to complete the sentences:

talk   school   home   help   teacher

6) I feel safe with people who can _____ me.

7) When I am worried, it is good to _____ to a friend.

8) I can be a good helper at _____ and at _____.

9) My _____ can help me when I have a problem.

Draw or Write

10) Who can you go to for help?

we are
a safe
& caring
school.

DECEMBER
Respect Yourself and Others

- **Acceptance**
- **Respect**
- **Manners**

- **Communication Skills**
- **Helping Others**
- **Inclusion**

Belonging to a community means getting along with others, having a special place to be together, and understanding the expectations of the group's members. It is important for children to understand that as active participants of their school community, they are expected to help create a safe and caring environment. The more we teach children to get along, the better and more productive citizens they will become.

MONTHLY OBJECTIVES
Students will:

- learn specific ways they can be responsible members of their school community
- practice using good manners to show respect

TEACHING TIPS

- Teaching the golden rule is a priority in a safe and caring environment. To teach children to care about others, first teach them to care and value themselves.
- A key ingredient to caring about others is having empathy—*the ability to understand, predict, and relate to someone's feelings*. Without empathy, children will have a difficult time resolving problems in peaceful ways. If we cultivate empathy in young children, it will become a natural feeling as they grow older.
- Model empathy and the golden rule as often as possible.

DECEMBER INTEGRATED ACTIVITIES

In addition to the specific lesson plans for this month, you can use these optional ideas to integrate and extend the Safe & Caring themes into daily routines and across the curricular areas.

LANGUAGE ARTS

- Have students write and illustrate stories (or share them in circle time where you can write them as they are dictated) using key words from this month's theme. Have a special event (Author's Day) for students to share their work with parents and other special guests.

- Read *My Hands* by Aliki. Use the book to explore positive ways the children can use their hands each day. Create a classroom book that shows the many ways your students use their hands to help others.

LITERATURE

- Read *Jamaica's Find* by Juanita Havill. Students can work in small groups to create a summary of what they read. Include their interpretation of the story, what the characters did, and how they felt. Each group should plan to present its summary to the large group.

- Read *Seaweed Soup* by Stuart Murphy. Turtle decides to make soup and has to share it with a lot of friends. Discuss the concept of sharing.

SOCIAL STUDIES

- Students work in small groups to discuss and determine what their contributions will be to making school a safe and caring place.

- Read *The Ups and Downs of Simpson Snail* by John Himmelman. Discuss ways friends can be kind to one another.

ART

- Have students decorate a bulletin board or classroom door showing people using good manners.

- Have the children make and cut out handprints on colored construction paper. Write on each handprint a way they can make their school a caring place by doing respectful things. Post the handprints around the school, adding to the display more handprints as you catch kids being kind each day.

MUSIC

- Listen to songs about acceptance and friendship on *Music Is Awesome Volume 2* by Yo Gabba Gabba (www.yogabbagabba.com). Discuss the songs and how they teach us to respect each other.

MATH

- Use the Caring Hearts year-round activity (pages 9 and 87) to track the number of times good manners are used in your classroom on a daily basis. Start with a new tally every morning.

- Add a token to a jar for each act of kindness a student shows. Count the tokens at the end of the day and at the end of the week. Review the numbers with children, and be sure to celebrate.

Safe & Caring Schools Vocabulary Builder

LEARNING OBJECTIVES

Students will:

- be introduced to vocabulary that supports respecting themselves and others
- internalize the vocabulary as they use it throughout the month and year in real-life situations

MATERIALS NEEDED

"Safe & Caring Vocabulary Builder" activity sheet (page 83) and pencils

LESSON PLAN

Use the vocabulary activities to introduce the main themes of this month's topic. Throughout the month, use the words in writing, spelling, storytelling, and in teachable moments. Add the words to your word wall.

For the Word Find activity, choose to use the key words, challenge words, or both. Discuss what the words mean after completing the page. You may want students to work in pairs to help each other.

For the vocabulary exercise, select words from the list to complete the sentences. The sentences will read:

- The *golden* rule tells us to *respect* others.
- Say *please* and *thank-you* when you ask for something.
- Good *manners* help us get along.
- Rumors are not the same as the *truth*.

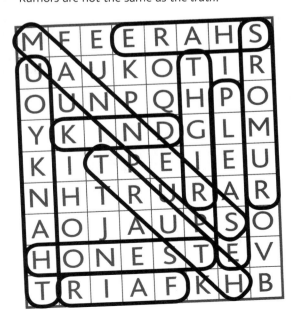

I Respect Others

LEARNING OBJECTIVES

Students will:

- learn about respectful behavior
- see that respect is part of good manners

MATERIALS NEEDED

The book *I'm Like You, You're Like Me* by Cindy Gainer, copies of "I Respect Others" activity sheet (page 84), and pencils or pens

LESSON PLAN

READ *I'm Like You, You're Like Me*. This book presents the concept of diversity with language children can understand: hair may be straight or curly, families may have many or few people, bodies may be big or small and each is unique.

> An optional text for teacher shared reading is *I Did It, I'm Sorry* by Caralyn Buehner. In a multiple-choice format, a guessing game deals with ethical dilemmas faced by animal characters.

DISCUSS Begin by reviewing the meaning of the golden rule *(treat others the way you want to be treated, with respect)*. Explain to children that when they use their good manners, they are choosing to treat others with respect. Ask children to give you examples of how people show respect to each other *(paying attention when someone is speaking, not interrupting, not pushing, not using unkind words)*.

DO the "I Respect Others" activity sheet. If you want to do this as a class activity, make an overhead transparency of the worksheet. Students determine if a specific behavior is respectful or disrespectful. Then, they draw their own pictures of how they can choose to show respect.

RELATE using good manners to showing respect for others. During circle time, model the kind words and actions that children can use throughout the day.

Practice Your Manners

LEARNING OBJECTIVES

Students will:

- understand what good manners are and why they are important
- review words and actions that are polite and respectful

MATERIALS NEEDED

The book *Mind Your Manners: In School* by Arianna Candell, "Practice Your Manners" activity sheet (page 85), and pencils or pens

LESSON PLAN

READ   *Mind Your Manners: In School*. Brief stories describe classroom friendships, the importance of silence when the teacher is giving a lesson, the friendly way for borrowing and sharing, picking up toys after playtime, and other typical school situations.

An optional text for teacher shared reading is *Perfect Pigs* by Marc Brown and Stephen Krensky. This is an introduction to good manners with family and friends, at school, during meals, with pets, on the phone, while playing games, at parties, and in public places.

DISCUSS   Define good manners. When we choose to be polite, we show people that we care. Brainstorm what to say and do that show good manners (using please and thank you, holding a door open for someone, offering to help with a chore, respecting the feelings of others).

DO   the "Practice Your Manners" activity sheet. Ask students to draw a line to match the "good manners" phrase with the situation in which they would use it. This activity may be done as a whole class by making an overhead transparency of the activity sheet.

RELATE   the importance of good manners to life in the classroom. Tell the children they will get along better, and feel happier, if they use good manners while playing and working. Have children role-play the words and actions they can use to show good manners in different school situations.

Good Manners or Bad Manners

LEARNING OBJECTIVES

Students will:

- learn that safe and caring people are concerned about their manners
- differentiate between good and bad manners

MATERIALS NEEDED

The book *It's a Spoon, Not a Shovel* by Caralyn Buehner, "Good Manners or Bad Manners" activity sheet (page 86), and crayons or markers

LESSON PLAN

READ   *It's a Spoon, Not a Shovel*. Victor Vulture, Crocodile Jones, and their friends demonstrate the right and wrong things to do in this humorous guide to proper manners.

An optional text for teacher shared reading is *Oops! Excuse Me Please! And Other Mannerly Tales* by Bob McGrath. This is a collection of 28 vignettes illustrating good manners, such as proper etiquette, following the golden rule, and memorizing correct phrases.

DISCUSS   Use examples from the book to review how good manners relate to what we say and do. Discuss the kinds of manners used in a safe and caring classroom and why they are important for learning and social development.

DO   the "Good Manners or Bad Manners" activity sheet. Help those who can't read all the words, or have the children work in pairs, with a good reader in each pair.

RELATE   the activity to real life within the classroom. How can good manners keep the classroom safe and caring? In circle time, share the completed activity sheets and close with the "Safe & Caring Promise" from the September activities (page 26).

Don't Put Up with Put-Downs

LEARNING OBJECTIVES

Students will:

- define and identify *put-downs* and the effect they have

- choose alternatives to using put-downs and negative responses

MATERIALS NEEDED

The book *Whoopi's Big Book of Manners* by Whoopi Goldberg, "Safe & Caring Hearts" activity sheet (page 87), craft sticks for puppets, scissors, poster board, glue, and tape

LESSON PLAN

READ   *Whoopi's Big Book of Manners.* This book reminds readers of polite phrases to use every day, such as please and thank you. It also teaches kids to pay attention to their manners mistakes *(interrupting, forgetting to clean up after yourself, not saying you're sorry)* and to practice politeness.

> An optional text for teacher shared reading is *Princess Penelope's Parrot* by Helen Lester. Spoiled Princess Penelope cannot get her new parrot to talk, even after threatening it and calling it nasty names. In a fun and fitting conclusion, the parrot gets revenge on the greedy princess.

DISCUSS   Review Stop, Think, Choose and I-messages activities from October (pages 52 and 53). What is a put-down? How do you know when someone puts you down? How does it make you feel? What is the opposite of a put-down? How does a "put-up" make you feel?

DO   the "Safe & Caring Hearts" activity to make stick puppets for use throughout the year. You may want to make a couple sets of puppets for the classroom or you may have each student make her or his own set. Cut out the hearts from the "Safe & Caring Hearts" activity sheet. Laminate the hearts or glue them to poster board before taping them to craft sticks. Use the heart puppets to role-play the difference between put-downs and put-ups. Ask the children if they know what happened to the first puppet (the one with the bandage). They may say the heart is sad or broken. What can they do to make the heart happy? Have children help the puppets deal with a conflict. Call for suggestions from the students on how the puppets can resolve the problem in a caring way.

RELATE   the lesson to what the children say or hear on a daily basis. Remind them that sometimes we hurt people's feelings by the things we say and do. If we hurt people's feelings, they won't want to be our friends. This is an opportunity to explore the concept of consequences. When reading stories in class, have the kids use the heart puppets to indicate if a character's action was or wasn't a safe and caring thing to do.

Thumbs Up or Thumbs Down

LEARNING OBJECTIVES

Students will:

- review safe and caring vocabulary words

- distinguish between good and bad behaviors

MATERIALS NEEDED

The book *Talk and Work It Out* by Cheri J. Meiners, "Thumbs Up or Down" activity sheet (page 88), and pencils or pens

LESSON PLAN

READ   *Talk and Work It Out.* Children learn that they can choose words that are helpful instead of hurtful to solve problems.

> An optional text for teacher shared reading is *Be Polite and Kind* by Cheri J. Meiners. A boy talks about showing others, through his words and actions, that they are important to him. He treats others with respect and wants to be treated the same.

DISCUSS   concepts from the book that help resolve conflicts in a positive way. Help children understand they can choose kind words that help them get along with others. Choosing to use unkind words hurts people's feelings.

DO   the "Thumbs Up or Down" activity sheet. Children circle the thumbs-up or the thumbs-down to indicate if the words are helping or hurting words. This activity may be done as a whole group activity by making an overhead transparency of the activity sheet.

RELATE   the golden rule to the kind words and actions the kids can use daily. The golden rule gives children a sense of empowerment when they know they have a part in creating and maintaining their safe and caring school.

Good Manners Flower

LEARNING OBJECTIVES

Students will:

- identify different ways to show respect
- practice positive talk

MATERIALS NEEDED

The book *Please Say Please! Penguin's Guide to Manners* by Margery Cuyler, "Good Manners Flower" activity sheet (page 89), crayons or markers, scissors, glue, and construction paper

LESSON PLAN

READ *Please Say Please! Penguin's Guide to Manners*. This book reinforces polite behavior by showing what not to do. Animal friends come to Penguin's house for dinner. They have terrible table manners, and the reader is asked to consider their conduct.

> An optional text for teacher shared reading is *Mrs. Peloki's Substitute* by Joanne Oppenheim. When a substitute teacher comes to Mrs. Peloki's classroom, nobody remembers their manners.

DISCUSS Ask children what happens when they forget their manners. Discuss how important it is to use good manners at all times, especially when they are visitors or guests. Review how the animals behaved in the story. What did the students learn from the story?

DO the "Good Manners Flower" activity. Each child will create a flower by cutting out the petals and the stem and assembling them on a sheet of construction paper. To reinforce practicing good manners, create a large classroom garden on a bulletin board. When children are caught using good manners, give them individual petals to add to the garden's flowers. Watch the garden grow!

RELATE practicing good manners to the classroom climate. Display the "Good Manners Flowers" as reminders to use good manners every day.

Kind Hand

LEARNING OBJECTIVES

Students will:

- discuss various uses for their hands
- identify ways they can be responsible members of their school community

MATERIALS NEEDED

The book *Hands Are Not for Hitting* by Martine Agassi, crayons or markers, pencils or pens, scissors, construction paper, and a digital camera (optional)

LESSON PLAN

READ *Hands Are Not for Hitting*. This book is written for younger children, but still offers clear alternatives to hitting and hurtful behavior that apply to older students. Use the book as a guide to peaceful and positive outcomes when students interact with each other.

> An optional text for teacher shared reading is *I Call My Hand Gentle* by Amanda Haan. The book presents things a hand can do: pick up things, throw, hold, write, draw, push. Then, the book moves to bigger issues, such as honorable behaviors and choices ("I choose not to steal, push, hurt").

DISCUSS Review the different things hands can do. Brainstorm ways to help make school a safe and caring place *(be good helpers, be good listeners, keep hands to ourselves, use kind words, be friends)*.

DO a visual reminder of helping hands by having the children trace their hands on construction paper and cut out the drawings. In the center of their handprints, have students draw pictures of themselves or write their names. If you have a digital camera and printer, you may want to take the children's pictures to use in the hands. On each finger, have the children write one thing they can do to make their school safe and caring. Help with the spelling of words as needed. Attach the hands together to make a border to decorate the classroom.

RELATE Using the caring actions on the handprints, discuss what it means for students to be responsible for their own actions. Tell students that hands are meant for helping others, too, and that it's important to know they can depend on each other all year long.

I Did Not Do It!

LEARNING OBJECTIVES

Students will:

- understand how important it is to be responsible for their own actions
- discuss how it feels to be blamed for something they have not done

MATERIALS NEEDED

The book *It Wasn't My Fault* by Helen Lester, "I Did Not Do It!" activity sheet (page 90), pens, pencils, markers, and posterboard

LESSON PLAN

READ   *It Wasn't My Fault.* Young Murdley Gurdson suddenly has an egg laid on his head. The bird claims, "It wasn't my fault," so Murdley sets out on a humorous adventure to discover where the fault lies.

An optional text for teacher shared reading is *It Wasn't Me! Telling the Truth* by Brian Moses. This book makes it clear that telling a lie is usually a lot worse than whatever you did wrong in the first place. The author shows how lies grow and spread quickly.

DISCUSS   Review what happened in the story. What did Murdley want to find out? Why did it take so long? What did the other animals do when asked about what happened? Discuss what it means to be responsible for your own actions. Ask the children who is responsible for the things they say and do. This is an important time to help them understand that their actions are a result of their choices.

DO   the "I Did Not Do It!" activity sheet. Ask children to either draw a picture or write about a time they were blamed for something they did not do, or about a time they blamed someone else, or a make-believe story about blaming.

RELATE   telling the truth about what you do to how it feels to be blamed for something you did not do. Review the concept of being responsible for your own actions. Close with the promise that everyone will try their best not to blame others for something they have done.

Playing Fair

LEARNING OBJECTIVES

Students will:

- learn the importance of playing fair
- practice the steps for playing fair

MATERIALS NEEDED

The book *Join In and Play* by Cheri J. Meiners, "Playing Fair" activity sheet (page 91), crayons or markers

LESSON PLAN

READ   *Join In and Play.* A girl explains what she does and says when she wants to play with someone. The story gives options when things don't work out as expected, emphasizing the importance of talking and listening with respect and playing fair.

An optional text for teacher shared reading is *Playing Fair* by Shelly Neilsen, Rosemary Wallner, and Virginia Kylberg. Brief rhymes present occasions when fairness is needed in dealing with friends, bullies, games, groups, or tests.

DISCUSS   the book you read. Brainstorm to make a list of what friends need to do to get along during playtime. *(The list may include follow the rules, wait for your turn, use kind words, ask for what you need, and no fighting.)*

DO   the "Playing Fair" activity sheet. Students decide if the situation is fair or unfair and color the corresponding face. Then have students draw a picture of playing fair with their friends.

RELATE   fairness to why we have rules. How does fairness affect games we play with our friends? What happens if someone does not play fair or treat everyone fairly? What would happen if games didn't have rules? Have students share their pictures about playing fair.

It's the Truth

LEARNING OBJECTIVES

Students will:

- learn the meaning of honesty
- discuss why honesty is important

MATERIALS NEEDED

The book *I'm Telling the Truth: A First Look at Honesty* by Pat Thomas, "It's the Truth" activity sheet (page 92), and pencils or pens

LESSON PLAN

READ *I'm Telling the Truth: A First Look at Honesty*. Children are shown that although being honest can be hard, it is worth it. Kids learn that when they all practice being honest, the world becomes a fairer and happier place to live.

An optional text for teacher shared reading is *A Big Fat Enormous Lie* by Marjorie Weinman Sharmat. A child's simple lie grows to enormous proportions.

DISCUSS the consequences of not telling the truth. How do people feel when someone is not being honest with them?

DO the "It's the Truth" activity sheet. Students fill in the speech bubbles for the child telling a lie about what happened and then telling the truth. Help the children fill in the blanks for the definition of honesty.

RELATE the theme of the lesson to real life by making a connection between honesty, respect, and good manners. Create a "Wall of Honesty" where students can display the Caring Hearts they receive every time they get caught being honest.

Let's Be Honest

LEARNING OBJECTIVES

Students will:

- define honesty
- determine what it means to be dishonest

MATERIALS NEEDED

The book *Jamaica and the Substitute Teacher* by Juanita Havill, "Let's Be Honest" activity sheet (page 93), and pencils or pens

LESSON PLAN

READ *Jamaica and the Substitute Teacher*. When it's time for the spelling test, Jamaica realizes that she's forgotten to study, so she copies from a friend.

An optional text for teacher shared reading is *Honest Ashley* by Virginia Kroll. A girl must choose between doing her own paper for school or reusing a paper that her brother did for the same assignment several years earlier. Reading her brother's story about honesty forces her to think hard about doing the right thing.

DISCUSS Why did Jamaica copy the answers from a friend? How did she feel when she got a perfect score? What did she choose to do? What did the teacher say and do?

DO the "Let's Be Honest" activity sheet. Students decide if the words relate to being honest or dishonest. Then they do math problems to decide which words to write in the blanks to complete the sentences. Finally, they write a definition for honesty.

RELATE the key points of the story you read to real-life situations the students experience at school or at home. Discuss the difference between honesty and tactfulness.

Respect Yourself and Others Quiz

Use the quiz activity sheet (page 94) to review and assess what the students learned this month. *(Answers: 1-T, 2-F, 3-T, 4-F, 5-T, 6-wait, 7-thank you, 8-honest, 9-manners)*

SAFE & CARING
VOCABULARY BUILDER

Word Find

M	F	E	E	R	A	H	S
U	A	U	K	O	T	I	R
O	U	N	P	Q	H	P	O
Y	K	I	N	D	G	L	M
K	I	T	P	E	I	E	U
N	H	T	R	U	R	A	R
A	O	J	A	U	P	S	O
H	O	N	E	S	T	E	V
T	R	I	A	F	K	H	B

Circle these words in the Word Find puzzle.
(Hint: Words can run up, down, forward, backward, or diagonally.)

Key Words:
FAIR
RIGHT
KIND
SHARE
TRUTH

Challenge Words:
HONEST
MANNERS
PLEASE
THANK YOU
RUMORS

Use these words to fill in the blanks:
thank you, truth, golden, manners, please, respect

The _____ rule tells us to _____ others.

Say _____ and _____ when you ask for something.

Good _____ help us get along with each other.

Rumors are not the same as the _____.

we are
a safe
& caring
school.

DECEMBER

I RESPECT OTHERS

Are these respectful or disrespectful ways to act?

	Respectful	Disrespectful
Being polite.	⬭	⬭
Name-calling.	⬭	⬭
Helping clean up a mess.	⬭	⬭
Stealing other people's things.	⬭	⬭
Being a bully.	⬭	⬭
Cutting in line.	⬭	⬭
Asking permission.	⬭	⬭
Apologizing for mistakes.	⬭	⬭
Saying thank you.	⬭	⬭

Here's how I show respect.

we aRe a SaFe & CaRiNG SCHOOL.

PRACTICE YOUR MANNERS

How are you?

What you say when you ask for something.

May I?

What you say when someone gives you something or does something nice for you.

Please.

What you say when you interrupt or bump into someone.

Thank you.

What you say when you want to know how someone feels.

No thank you.

Excuse me.

What you say when you want to do something.

What you say when someone offers you something you don't want.

I'm sorry.

What you say when you have done something wrong.

we are a safe & caring school.

GOOD MANNERS OR BAD MANNERS

 GOOD Manners    **BAD Manners**

  1) Saying "hello" when you meet someone

 2) Shaking hands

 3) Tattling to get someone in trouble

   4) Helping a friend

 5) Opening a door for someone

 6) Using unkind words

   7) Waiting your turn

8) Interrupting someone who is speaking

 9) Caring about people's feelings

 10) Hitting or pushing when angry

 11) Spitting

 12) Helping with chores

 13) Calling names when upset

 14) Saying "please" and "thank you"

we are a safe & caring school.

Safe & Caring Hearts

THUMBS UP OR DOWN

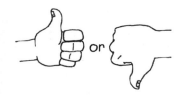 or compliments

 or kindness

 or bossy

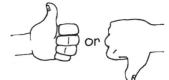 or sharing

 or put-downs

 or put-ups

 or fighting

 or pushing

 or listening

 or taking turns

 or good manners

 or helper

 or cooperating

 or caring

 or kind words

 or teasing

we aRe a safe & CaRiNG SCHOOL.

GOOD MANNERS FLOWER

Excuse me.

Can I help?

Thank you.

I am sorry.

May I?

Please?

WE ARE
a SAFE
& CARING
SCHOOL.

Draw + Write

I DID NOT DO IT!

Have you ever been blamed for something you didn't do? Have you ever blamed someone else? What happened? How was the problem solved?

PLAYING FAIR

Color the face to show if each action is fair or unfair.

	Fair	Unfair
Wait for my turn	☺	☹
Yell	☺	☹
Grab	☺	☹
Use my kind words	☺	☹
Ask to join the game	☺	☹
Argue	☺	☹
Follow the rules	☺	☹
Push and shove	☺	☹
Always go first	☺	☹

Draw a picture of playing fair with your friends.

we are
a safe
& caring
school.

IT'S THE TRUTH

Write what the boy would say if he was telling a LIE.

Write what the boy would say if he was telling the TRUTH.

Use these words to fill in the blanks: **trust, tell, truth.**

Honesty means telling the _____.

When we _____ the truth,

people will _____ us.

we aRe
a safe
& CaRiNG
SCHOOL.

LET'S BE HONEST

Solve the math problems and use the answers to complete the sentences below.

Define honest: _____

_____

_____

Read each word.
Decide if it describes being honest (happy face) or being dishonest (sad face).

lie

sneak

truth

cheat

right choice

responsible

steal

trick

trust

1 + 2 = _____ **honest**   4 – 2 = _____ **safe**

3 – 2 = _____ **good**   10 + 10 = _____ **helps**

5 + 5 = _____ **truth**   7 – 3 = _____ **school**

It is _____ (1) to be _____ (3) .

The _____ (10) _____ (20) us get

along in our _____ (2) and caring _____ (4) .

From *Activities for Building Character and Social-Emotional Learning Grades 1–2* by Katia S. Petersen, Ph.D., copyright © 2012. Free Spirit Publishing Inc., Minneapolis, MN; 800-735-7323; www.freespirit.com.
This page may be reproduced for individual, classroom, and small group work only. For all other uses, contact www.freespirit.com/company/permissions.cfm.

RESPECT YOURSELF AND OTHERS QUIZ

True or False (circle the correct answer)

1) I should show respect for others. .... **True / False**

2) When someone else is mean to me,
   I should be mean back. .... **True / False**

3) Playing fair helps me get along with others. .... **True / False**

4) Blaming others is funny. .... **True / False**

5) Saying "please" is good manners. .... **True / False**

Fill in the Blanks

Use these words to complete the sentences:

thank you   honest   wait   manners

6) It is important to _____ for my turn.

7) Say "please" and "_____ _____."

8) Telling the truth means being _____.

9) Respect others and use good _____.

Draw or Write

10) How can you show respect to someone else?

We Are
a safe
& caring
school.

JANUARY
Caring About One Another—Bullying

- **Empathy**
- **Respecting Others**

- **Bullying**
- **Teasing**
- **Being a Positive Bystander**

In a world where conflict, violence, drugs, and weapons have a daily presence, the ability to empathize is vital. Children who lack the skills of empathy and compassion may have difficulty with impulse control, which leads to conflict. The wrong look, a side comment, or an accidental push can quickly result in a major confrontation. With the appropriate skills, the magnitude of conflicts can be reduced. When we model empathy, our children will learn to care.

MONTHLY OBJECTIVES
Students will:

- work on accepting people for who they really are, not what they look like or appear to be
- practice empathetic skills
- learn the importance of compassion and kindness
- being a positive bystander

TEACHING TIPS

- At times, children will complain that we do not really hear what they are trying to tell us. Listen not only with your ears but also with your heart. When you listen with your heart, you are better able to understand the subtle yet important messages children are giving.

- Be proactive in anticipating negative conflict among students, which disrupts teaching and the students' ability to learn.

JANUARY INTEGRATED ACTIVITIES

In addition to the specific lesson plans for this month, you can use these optional ideas to integrate and extend the Safe & Caring themes into daily routines and across the curricular areas.

LANGUAGE ARTS

- Have students develop pen pals with elders in the community. Get names of potential pen pals and discuss logistics with a volunteer coordinator in your school, community organization, or church.

- Use an overhead transparency to write a story about bullying. Explain the topic and start the story by writing the opening sentence on the transparency. Let each student provide a sentence that relates to the main idea while you write it on the transparency. Talk about using descriptive words in the writing (adjectives and adverbs). When the story is done, transfer it from the transparency to paper. Then allow the children to add illustrations to the story.

- Students can write short stories about bullying and share them with the class.

LITERATURE

- Read the book *The Brave Little Parrot* by Rafe Martin. This is a traditional Indian *jataka* tale. A brave gray parrot labors against a forest fire and the gods reward him with colorful feathers. Talk about the importance of helping in tough situations.

- Read stories about children or young people who have courage, like *Courage of the Blue Boy* by Robert Neubecker. This is a story about a boy who tries to fit in while staying true to himself. Another story to read is *Arnie and the Skateboard Gang* by Nancy Carlson. Discuss how Arnie makes the right choice when challenged to do a dangerous thing.

- Define and discuss *empathy, diversity,* and *bullying.* Provide children's newspapers or magazines to search for stories or articles about empathy, diversity, and bullying.

SOCIAL STUDIES

- Read *Martin's Big Words: The Life of Dr. Martin Luther King, Jr.* by Doreen Rappaport. Discuss Dr. King's character traits. Each week explore a trait such as compassion, equality, empathy, acceptance, and kindness.

- Read stories about kindness. Ask students to draw pictures that show ways people can be kind to one another.

ART

- Using caring as a theme, decorate a bulletin board near the entrance of the school or in another common area of the school.

- Make paper-bag puppets of characters from the stories read and use them to retell the story.

- Help students create kindness cards to give to home-bound people. Send cards to a local nursing home.

MUSIC

- Listen to songs from the CD *Can Cockatoos Count by Twos?* by Hap Palmer (www.happalmer.com). Discuss the lyrics or do the related activity listed at the website.

MATH

- Read *Super Sand Castle Saturday* by Stuart J. Murphy. Three friends compete to see who can build the tallest sand castle, the deepest moat, and the longest wall. When they start to measure, trouble begins because each friend uses a different nonstandard unit of measurement.

Safe & Caring Schools Vocabulary Builder

LEARNING OBJECTIVES

Students will:

- be introduced to vocabulary that supports learning how to care for others and diffuse bullying situations
- internalize the vocabulary as they use it throughout the month and year in real-life situations

MATERIALS NEEDED

"Safe & Caring Vocabulary Builder" activity sheet (page 103) and pencils

LESSON PLAN

Use the vocabulary activity sheet to introduce the concepts and common language of this month's theme. Throughout the month, use the words in writing, spelling, storytelling, and dealing with bullying situations. Add the words to your word wall.

For the Word Find activity, choose to use the key words, challenge words, or both. Discuss what the words mean after completing the page. You may want students to work in pairs to help each other.

For the fill-in-the-blanks activity, students add the letters to complete the words *(bully, feelings, tell, sorry, friend, hurt, bossy,* and *hit)*.

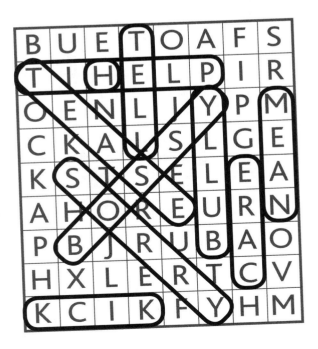

People Packages

LEARNING OBJECTIVES

Students will:

- learn there is more to a person than what they see on the outside
- understand the importance of respecting individuality

MATERIALS NEEDED

The book *Different Just Like Me* by Lori Mitchell, paper lunch bags (one per child), writing paper, construction paper, pencils or pens, crayons, markers, and glue

LESSON PLAN

READ *Different Just Like Me*. A little girl and her mother go on daily errands and always encounter someone who is different—someone who is either older, speaks another language, has a disability, or is of a different race—but doing the same thing as the little girl.

> An optional text for teacher shared reading is *Friends at School* by Rochelle Bunnett. Even though some children may look different and have different abilities, all children like to do the same things.

DISCUSS the fact that people come in all sizes, shapes, and colors, and with different abilities and backgrounds. Talk about how sometimes we judge people by looking at them from the outside, rather than getting to know them on the inside. Inside, we have thoughts and feelings that make us unique and interesting people.

DO Make "People Packages" in order to explore similarities and differences among classmates. On slips of paper, the students draw or write things that describe themselves, such as a favorite book, things they enjoy doing, favorite foods, favorite colors, their talents, or number of people in their family. Have each child place the drawings or notes inside a paper bag. Using construction paper or other art supplies, students can construct their faces and bodies to glue on the outside of the bags.

RELATE today's lesson to the adage, "You can't tell a book by its cover." What do the children think this means? Have them take turns naming the things in their bags during circle time. Draw attention to the similarities in the group as well as the differences. Emphasize that regardless of differences, everyone has feelings and deserves to be treated with kindness and respect.

What Is Bullying?

LEARNING OBJECTIVES

Students will:

- be introduced to the issue of bullying
- identify what bullying looks like, sounds like, and feels like

MATERIALS NEEDED

The book *Being Bullied* by Kate Petty, "What Is Bullying?" activity sheet (page 104), and pencils or pens

LESSON PLAN

READ *Being Bullied*. Rita is bullied by another girl at school but finds relief when she stands up for herself.

An optional text for teacher shared reading is *Tattlin' Madeline* by Carol Cummings. It teaches young children the difference between tattling and reporting. Written in rhyme to read aloud or for guided reading, it provides repeated word patterns and predictable text.

DISCUSS Review the different kinds of bullying introduced in the story. Ask children to identify the feelings mentioned. Discuss the types of bullying *(physical, verbal, emotional)*, where bullying usually happens, the characteristics of bullies, and why people bully others. Explain that bullying always hurts someone and that some form of it happens frequently.

DO the "What Is Bullying?" activity sheet. Students determine if an action is bullying or not. The activity sheet can be copied on a transparency and used as a class activity on an overhead projector. Discuss how students responded to the final question.

RELATE the lesson to life within school. Make the point that bullying is not acceptable. Review the completed activity sheets. Talk about what individual students can do to help stop bullying. Encourage children who are bullied, or see bullying, to ask for help from people they know and trust.

Different but the Same

LEARNING OBJECTIVES

Students will:

- review the concepts of similar and different
- learn that everyone deserves to feel included, regardless of their differences

MATERIALS NEEDED

The book *All the Colors of the Earth* by Sheila Hamanaka, "Different but the Same" activity sheet (page 105), pens or pencils, and markers or crayons

LESSON PLAN

READ *All the Colors of the Earth*. Lyrical text and colorful paintings celebrate the earth, children, and the ethnic diversity of the world's people.

An optional text for teacher shared reading is *I'm Like You, You're Like Me* by Cindy Gainer. Illustrations and simple text explore ways in which children are alike and different to help kids understand and celebrate each other.

DISCUSS Review how wonderful each of us is and how we all deserve to feel included, regardless of our differences. Children must first learn to accept themselves before they can learn to accept others.

DO the "Different but the Same" activity sheet. Students work in teams of two to complete the activity. Partners take turns drawing a picture of each other. Encourage the children to pay attention to details, such as type of hair, freckles, shape of nose, glasses, and color of eyes.

RELATE the lesson to real life by looking at the diversity within the classroom, school, or community. Everyone is different, but everyone belongs. During group time, ask the children to share what they discovered about each other. Remind them we are more alike than different. Understanding our differences not only helps us get along, it makes our world a much more interesting and fun place.

Bully Problems

LEARNING OBJECTIVES

Students will:

- learn to identify bullying behaviors
- discover practical, nonviolent ways to deal with bullies

MATERIALS NEEDED

The book *King of the Playground* by Phyllis Reynolds Naylor, "Bully Problems" activity sheet (page 106), pens, pencils, markers, and posterboard

LESSON PLAN

READ *King of the Playground.* Kevin gets help from his dad to overcome his fear of a bully who is intimidating him on the playground.

> An optional text for teacher shared reading is *Simon's Hook: A Story About Teases and Put-Downs* by Karen Gedig Burnett. When his friends tease him, Simon rushes home in tears. He finds consolation when his grandmother tells him "a fish story" that illustrates the pitfalls of providing an easy target for teasing by "biting the hook."

DISCUSS all the bullying behaviors in the story *(pushing, yelling, etc.)*. Help children identify feelings people experience when they are bullied. How does Kevin feel when he goes back to the playground to face Sammy? What advice did Kevin's father give him? What can Kevin do about the bully?

DO the "Bully Problems" activity sheet. Children draw or write a story about bullies. If the children do not wish to share a personal experience, they can retell the story you read about bullies. The goal is to process how to deal with bullies.

RELATE Reinforce the fact that it is never fun to be bullied, and it is never okay to hurt people just to get what we want. Have the children share their pictures or stories. Discuss options for dealing with kids who bully. It is important for the children to know that they might not always be able to solve bullying problems alone. Encourage them to ask for help from an adult they know and trust.

What to Do About Being Bossy

LEARNING OBJECTIVES

Students will:

- use kind words and actions to deal with bossy friends
- learn strategies to deal with difficult situations

MATERIALS NEEDED

The book *Bootsie Barker Bites* by Barbara Bottner, "What to Do About Being Bossy" activity sheet (page 107), pencils or pens, and crayons or markers

LESSON PLAN

READ *Bootsie Barker Bites.* Bootsie Barker is a girl who likes to kick dogs, throw temper tantrums, stick out her tongue, and only play rough games—until her friend finds a better way to get along and have fun.

> An optional text for teacher shared reading is *The Ugly Duckling* by Hans Christian Andersen. This is the classic tale of the large, ugly duckling that suffers greatly, but grows to be a beautiful swan.

DISCUSS the idea that some children choose to be bossy to get their way. Why did Bootsie Barker choose to be bossy? How did the other child feel? What can friends do to help each other when someone is being bossy? Point out how hard it is to make or keep friends when we are bossy.

DO the "What to Do About Being Bossy" activity sheet. Students draw a picture of a time they experienced dealing with a bossy friend. If children choose not to share a personal experience, suggest that they draw the conflict from the story you read.

RELATE making good and bad choices to dealing with bossy friends. How can we help bossy friends make better choices?

Stop the Tease Monster Game

LEARNING OBJECTIVES

Students will:

- learn to identify teasing behaviors
- realize that teasing hurts feelings

MATERIALS NEEDED

The book *Oliver Button Is a Sissy* by Tomie de Paola and "Stop the Tease Monster" activity sheet template (page 108)

LESSON PLAN

READ   *Oliver Button Is a Sissy.* Oliver Button would rather read, dance, and draw pictures than play football like the other boys. His classmates tease him, but his persistence pays off in the end.

DISCUSS   how Oliver Button is teased by others. How do you think Oliver felt about being teased? Explain to the children that teasing can make people feel bad. If we respect each other, we do not tease. Kidding is having fun with someone in a way that does not hurt his or her feelings. Unlike kidding, teasing is a put-down because it makes fun of someone.

DO   Play the "Stop the Tease Monster" game. Cut out the three "Stop the Tease Monster" cards from the activity sheet so every child has a set. You may want to laminate these for better durability. Read one of the five situations (that follow) to the class. The children decide if it is a teasing situation. If yes, they hold up the Tease Monster card. If no, they hold up the happy face. If it is a teasing situation, ask the class, "What should be done?" The first child with an answer shows the Stop, Think, Choose card. Call on the student to present the answer. Ask for other answers that students may offer.

Situations:

- Brian and Juan are telling everyone how much they can eat when they are hungry. When Jill brings cupcakes to class, Brian tells the class to be careful and keep Juan away because he might eat them all. Is it kidding or teasing?
- Tomas has to wear braces on his legs because of a bone condition. Jennifer envies him and calls him the "Bionic Boy" because he can stand for so long without having to sit down, like a robot. Is it kidding or teasing?
- In the same class, Jason is always calling Tomas a gimp and mimicking how he walks so stiffly. Is it kidding or teasing?
- Jessica is nicknamed "The Brain," because she is so smart. Is it kidding or teasing?
- Max bumps Aldin in the hall every day, causing him to drop his books. Max laughs and calls Aldin a klutz. Is it kidding or teasing?

RELATE   Ask the children to recap what they learned about teasing and kidding. Remind them that in their safe and caring school, they promised to respect each other, which means they care about each other and do not tease.

Tattling or Telling?

LEARNING OBJECTIVES

Students will:

- learn the difference between asking for help and tattling
- identify who can support them if they are being bullied

MATERIALS NEEDED

The book *Don't Squeal Unless It's a Big Deal* by Jeanie Franz Ransom, "Tattling or Telling?" activity sheet (page 109), and pencils or pens

LESSON PLAN

READ   *Don't Squeal Unless It's a Big Deal.* The piggies in Mrs. McNeal's class learn the difference between tattling and informing an adult in an emergency.

> An optional text for teacher shared reading is *A Bad Case of Tattle Tongue* by Julia Cook. No one likes "Josh the Tattler" because he tattles on his classmates, his brother, and even his dog. One night he awakens to find his tongue is very long, yellow, and covered in bright purple spots.

DISCUSS   what an emergency is and why it is okay to ask for help. Explain that tattling is meant to get someone in trouble, but asking for help is meant to alert an adult when help is needed. Give some examples and have students guess when it's tattling and when it's not. Review I-messages from the October lessons. Remind students to try working things out on their own first, but to ask for help when what they try does not work. In a dangerous or scary situation, it is always important to check in with a trusted adult immediately.

DO   the "Tattling or Telling?" activity sheet. Students review the four pictures and decide if they can solve the problem on their own or if they need to get help. If you choose to do this activity as a whole-class activity, make a transparency of the sheet to use on an overhead projector.

RELATE Review the difference between asking for help and tattling to get someone in trouble. Use the completed activity sheets to emphasize that bullying is never okay. Discuss how important it is to ask for help when being bullied or seeing someone else being bullied.

Caring Takes Courage

LEARNING OBJECTIVES

Students will:

- understand the meaning of courage
- learn that it takes courage to ask for help

MATERIALS NEEDED

The book *Believing Sophie* by Hazel Hutchins, "Caring Takes Courage" activity sheet (page 110), and pencils or pens

LESSON PLAN

READ *Believing Sophie*. Sophie is being accused of stealing, but she is able to stand up for herself and set things straight.

An optional text for teacher shared reading is *A Picture Book of Rosa Parks* by David A. Adler. Adler presents a simple, clear biography of Rosa Parks, exploring both her childhood and adult life. He makes it obvious that Parks' role in the civil rights movement did not begin and end on a bus, but rather lasted throughout her life.

DISCUSS Define *courage*. Make a list of situations when courage is needed to do something. *(List may include: trying a difficult activity or game, going to the dentist or doctor, saying the right thing, standing up for what's right, helping friends, being bullied, being blamed for something you did not do.)*

DO the "Caring Takes Courage" activity sheet. Students do the math problems (provide help as needed) to decide which words to use to fill in the blanks. Then they read each scenario and determine if the kids in the scene were being courageous. Finally, the students write what they would do if they were part of the situation.

RELATE courage to ways students can help each other stay safe. Remind them that you will be there to support them. Everyone deserves to feel safe.

What Can I Do About Bullies?

LEARNING OBJECTIVES

Students will:

- learn steps to help them deal with bullying behavior
- discover how to support one another in order to stay safe

MATERIALS NEEDED

The book *Loudmouth George and the Sixth-Grade Bully* by Nancy L. Carlson, "What Can I Do About Bullies?" activity sheet (page 111), pencils or pens

LESSON PLAN

READ *Loudmouth George and the Sixth-Grade Bully*. After having his lunch repeatedly stolen by a bully twice his size, Loudmouth George and his friend Harriet teach the bully a lesson he'll never forget.

An optional text for teacher shared reading is *The Story of Ruby Bridges* by Robert Coles. Ruby Bridges was the sole African American child to attend a New Orleans elementary school after court-ordered desegregation in 1960.

DISCUSS Remind students that bullying can be stopped if we help each other make better choices. No one deserves to be bullied or hurt in any way. Six steps to remember when faced with a bully: 1) Don't keep bullying a secret. 2) If you are being bullied, ask for help from someone you know and trust. 3) Use a strong voice to say how you feel. 4) Walk away. 5) Ignore the Bully. 6) Use "Stop, Think, Choose" to reach a solution.

DO Divide the class into four small groups. Give each group a scenario and have groups role-play the conflict and the solution.

- Two kids are excluding another kid from playing a game. What do the bystanders do?
- Two children are whispering and pointing a finger at another kid. What do the bystanders do?
- A bigger kid is pushing around a smaller kid. What do the bystanders do?
- One child is calling another "four eyes" because he wears glasses. What do the bystanders do?

Continue the activity by having the students complete the "What Can I Do About Bullies" activity sheet. Here they match a problem with an appropriate response. Discuss the choices when all have finished the sheet.

RELATE the role plays to life in school and on the playground. Demonstrate specific ways students can use I-messages (page 53) and Stop, Think, Choose (page 52) steps when they encounter a bully. Remind students that although it is not always easy to stand up to a bully, knowing what to do will help them.

Safe & Caring Schools Ambassadors of Peace

LEARNING OBJECTIVES

Students will:

- learn about the Ambassadors of Peace program
- explore how to behave as Ambassadors of Peace

MATERIALS NEEDED

The book *The Recess Queen* by Alexis O'Neill, "Safe & Caring Schools Ambassadors of Peace" activity sheet (page 112), and pencils or pens

LESSON PLAN

READ *The Recess Queen*. A schoolyard bully is enlightened by the new kid in class in this story about the power of kindness and friendship.

An optional text for teacher shared reading is *Big Al* by Andrew Clements. A big, ugly fish has trouble making the friends he longs for because of his appearance. That situation changes when his scary appearance saves them all from a fisherman's net.

DISCUSS Review what Ambassadors of Peace do to keep their school a safe place (page 8). Explain that everyone has the potential to be an Ambassador of Peace by helping to stop bullying behavior. Discuss real-life conflicts your students experience and help them find positive solutions. Explain that a positive bystander is one who steps in to help prevent bad things from happening or gets adults to help when needed.

DO the "Safe & Caring Schools Ambassadors of Peace" activity sheet. Have students, either individually or working in teams, read the conflict on the page and then write what they understand to be the problem (STOP), the options or choices to solve the problem (THINK), and the best solution (CHOOSE).

RELATE Talk about how you will identify and celebrate Ambassadors of Peace in your classroom and school. Tell the students they can all be ambassadors. Ask them to watch for situations where they can help one another.

Caring About One Another— Bullying Quiz

Use the quiz activity sheet (page 113) to review and assess what the students learned this month. *(Answers: 1-T, 2-F, 3-T, 4-T, 5-T, 6-fun, mean, 7-courage, 8-Peace, 9-accept)*

> *"In our Safe & Caring School we reach out to our children emotionally, so they feel they're in a safe, caring, nurturing environment where they're able to learn. They are encouraged to tell you their problems, so we can get past that hurdle and continue in the academic process."*
>
> **TEACHER, ARLINGTON SCHOOL**

SAFE & CARING
VOCABULARY BUILDER

Word Find

B	U	E	T	O	A	F	S		S
T	I	H	E	L	P	I	R		R
O	E	N	L	J	Y	P	M		M
C	K	A	L	S	L	G	E		E
K	S	T	S	E	L	E	A		A
A	H	O	R	E	U	R	N		N
P	B	J	R	U	B	A	O		O
H	X	L	E	R	T	C	V		V
K	C	I	K	F	Y	H	M		M

Circle these words in the Word Find puzzle.
(Hint: Words can run up, down, forward, backward, or diagonally.)

Key Words:
CARE
HIT
KICK
TELL
HELP

Challenge Words:
BULLY
TEASE
SORRY
BOSSY
MEAN

Complete the words by filling in the blanks.

bu _ _ y   _ o _ _ y   _ oss _

_ ee _ ing _   _ ri _ nd   h _ t

te _ _   _ u _ t

WE ARE
a SAFE
& CARING
SCHOOL.

WHAT IS BULLYING?

Bullies say or do things on purpose that hurt other people.

At our safe and caring school we treat each other with respect.

Put an X in the YES box if the action is bullying or in the NO box if it is not bullying.

YES	NO	
☐	☐	using put-downs
☐	☐	helping others
☐	☐	staying calm
☐	☐	walking away
☐	☐	saying how you feel

YES	NO	
☐	☐	tripping others
☐	☐	using threats
☐	☐	using compliments
☐	☐	asking for help
☐	☐	gossiping

YES	NO	
☐	☐	cooling down
☐	☐	talking things out
☐	☐	stealing
☐	☐	calling bad names
☐	☐	stop, think, choose

Describe a time when you were bullied. How did you feel? What did you do?

We are a safe & caring school.

Different But The Same

Me

You

we are
a safe
& caring
SCHOOL.

BULLY PROBLEMS

What's the problem?

How do I feel?

we are
a safe
& caring
SCHOOL.

What can I do?

WHAT TO DO ABOUT BEING BOSSY

we are a safe & caring SCHOOL.

Use these cut-outs for the Stop the Tease Monster Game.

STOP THE TEASE MONSTER

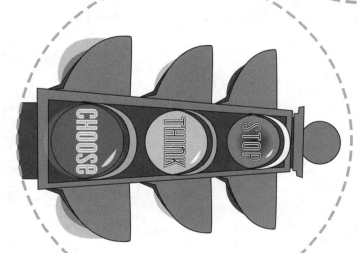

we are a safe & caring SCHOOL.

TATTLING OR TELLING?

1

Maria took Emily's lunch money.

What should we do?

Tell? YES NO

Who? _____
Why? _____

2

I saw Mark with a pencil just like the one Adam had.

What should we do?

Tell? YES NO

Who? _____
Why? _____

3

I heard Sam say he didn't like Joe.

What should we do?

Tell? YES NO

Who? _____
Why? _____

4

Sophie and Eric are fighting on the playground!

What should we do?

Tell? NO

Who? _____
Why? _____

We are a safe & caring school.

JANUARY

Caring Takes Courage

Let's see how courage works in real life!

Solve the math problems and use the answers to help fill in the blanks in the sentences below.

$10 + 2 =$ _____ **courage** $7 - 4 =$ _____ **safe**

$(12 + 6) - 4 =$ _____ **bullied** $5 - 1 =$ _____ **help**

$(25 - 19) + 5 =$ _____ **support**

When someone is being _____(14)_____ try to _____(4)_____. If it is not _____(3)_____ to help, remember to go to your safe and caring _____(11)_____ system. Getting help takes _____(12)_____, too!

	Was this courageous?	What would you do?
When Jimmy was being bullied by Mike and Pete, Joe got friends together to get Jimmy away from them.	Yes No	_____ _____ _____
When Jenny saw David and Carlos picking on Mario, she thought it was funny and joined in.	Yes No	_____ _____ _____
When LaShanda wouldn't let Shari join the game, Annette decided to play with Shari anyway.	Yes No	_____ _____ _____

we are a safe & caring SCHOOL.

Safe & Caring Schools
Ambassadors of Peace

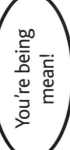

We can all be Ambassadors of Peace and help stop bullying at our school.

When kids act mean, what 3 steps can you take to help stop bullying?

That's not true.

You're being mean!

You guys don't know how to play ball! I'll just take the ball for myself.

1 **Stop**
What is the problem?

2 **Think**
What can be done about it?

3 **Choose**
What is the best choice?

we are a safe & caring school.

WHAT CAN I DO ABOUT BULLIES?

Match the problem with the best answer.

Two kids are excluding a third kid from the game they're playing.

Some girls are whispering and pointing at another girl close by.

You see a bully pushing a classmate around on the school bus.

One of your friends makes fun of a girl you don't know because she wears glasses.

Two teenagers take a bike away from a younger kid and won't give it back.

Ignore the bully.

Get a few friends together and stand up to the bully.

Say how you feel.

Ask an adult for help.

Tell your friend you don't like being mean to anyone.

Stand up for yourself.

Stop, Think, Choose.

Go over and make friends with the girl.

Go over and play a different game with the kid.

Walk away.

BONUS:
Stop, Think, Choose is ALWAYS a good answer!

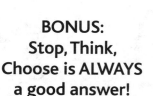
we aRe a saFe & CaRiNG SCHOOL.

CARING ABOUT ONE ANOTHER— BULLYING QUIZ

True or False (circle the correct answer)

1) Bullies can be very bossy. .... **True / False**

2) Telling is the same as tattling. .... **True / False**

3) Bullying is doing or saying things that hurt others. .... **True / False**

4) Our safe and caring school is a place where bullies
   are not allowed. .... **True / False**

5) Teasing hurts feelings. .... **True / False**

Fill in the Blanks

Unscramble these words to fill in the blanks and complete each sentence. (Hint: the first letter of the word is provided as a clue.)

acerogu   pactec   unf   aepec   emna

6) Kidding is **f**_____. Teasing is **m**_____.

7) When we stand up for what we believe we have **c**_____.

8) Ambassadors of **P**_____ help kids who are being bullied.

9) We **a**_____ others even though they may be different
   from us.

Draw or Write

10) How might you prevent bullying at your safe and caring school?

we are a safe & caring school.

" I think one of the most important things in a school is parent involvement. We've had a lack of parent involvement, but recently with Safe & Caring Schools we have promoted parent involvement through the Ambassadors of Peace breakfast. Every month we have a child from each class nominated as an Ambassador of Peace. We invite the parents to a special breakfast, and we celebrate with them and their children the accomplishments that the children have made. It's really a great way to have the parents come in and meet with the staff, and for parents to see that other parents are involved and that they do care."

COUNSELOR—TARBOX SCHOOL

FEBRUARY

Cooperation— Teaming Up for Success

- **Social Interaction Skills**
- **Responsibility**
- **Decision Making**

- **Teamwork**
- **Sharing**

Cooperation is the ability to work well with others in order to get things done. Children need to understand early on that cooperation is a valuable lifelong skill. They also need to learn that accountability, responsibility, being a good team player, and communicating effectively are all part of getting along.

MONTHLY OBJECTIVES
Students will:

- learn about responsibility and accountability
- experience leadership and teamwork skills
- practice communicating effectively with others

TEACHING TIPS

- Cooperation is one skill that takes time to teach. Being part of a team is not always easy for children. They have a hard time sharing, listening, taking turns, and following directions.
- There are valuable lessons children can learn while working in large or small groups. Explain to children that they have a right to their own opinions and feelings.
- Make it your goal to teach students how to communicate effectively and help them understand the power of teamwork.

FEBRUARY INTEGRATED ACTIVITIES

In addition to the specific lesson plans for this month, you can use these optional ideas to integrate and extend the Safe & Caring themes into daily routines and across the curricular areas.

LANGUAGE ARTS

- Have students write a story or make a list to describe the responsibilities of each family member at home.
- Review key words that focus on cooperation.

LITERATURE

- Read and discuss books based on the theme of cooperation. One option is to read *Swimmy* by Leo Lionni. Have the children use puppets to tell the story in their own words.
- Read books about the skills needed for cooperation. One example is *Because of You* by B.G. Hennessy. This book talks about sharing, listening, and paying attention. Discuss why students need to understand and practice being cooperative in order to get along at school.

SOCIAL STUDIES

- Invite community members and parents to be your special guests as career specialists. Ask them to share information about their particular responsibilities at work and how cooperation is a necessary part of being successful in a job. Help the students make a list of questions to ask before the guests arrive.

ART

- Have students draw pictures of the different responsibilities they have in the classroom. Collect all the pictures and create a bulletin board or book titled, "We Are a Team."
- Divide the class into small groups and ask each group to create a collage showing people cooperating. Give the students the option to draw pictures or find pictures in magazines or newspapers.
- Draw pictures of the many ways people communicate today.

MUSIC

- Listen to songs from *Turn on the Music* or *The Feel of Music* by Hap Palmer (www.happalmer.com). Discuss the song themes and lyrics with children.

MATH

- Divide the class into teams for a week. Give children a token each time they give a compliment to a team member or classmate. Each team will count their tokens at the end of the week to see how well the teams worked together.
- Read *Give Me Half!* by Stuart J. Murphy. Two siblings who cannot share anything, including responsibility, decide if they each do half of everything, life might be better.

"SCS lends itself easily to classroom use, it's so teacher-friendly. You can use it for whatever you might be doing—math, science, reading."

TEACHER, JOHN BREEN SCHOOL

Safe & Caring Schools Vocabulary Builder

LEARNING OBJECTIVES

Students will:

- be introduced to the vocabulary that supports learning how to be responsible for practicing cooperation
- internalize the vocabulary as they use it throughout the month and year in real-life situations

MATERIALS NEEDED

"Safe & Caring Vocabulary Builder" activity sheet (page 122) and pencils

LESSON PLAN

Use the vocabulary activities to introduce the concepts and common language associated with this month's theme. Throughout the month, use the words in writing, spelling, storytelling, and dealing with conflict situations. Add the words to your word wall.

For the Word Find activity, choose to use the key words, challenge words, or both. Discuss what the words mean after completing the page. You may want students to work in pairs to help each other.

For the fill-in-the-blanks activity, students fill in vowels to complete the words (*answer, ideas, team, secret, honest, finish*).

That's What I Like About You

LEARNING OBJECTIVES

Students will:

- understand that even the best of friends can have difficulty getting along at times
- learn that using kind words can be the greatest gift between friends

MATERIALS NEEDED

The book *Rosie and Michael* by Judith Viorst, "That's What I Like About You" activity sheet (page 123), craft sticks, scissors, two jars or two boxes

LESSON PLAN

READ *Rosie and Michael.* Rosie and Michael are best friends who share jokes, secrets, and fears. But sometimes even best friends don't get along.

> An optional story for teacher shared reading is *Grandmother's Dreamcatcher* by Becky Ray McCain. A Chippewa girl's bad dreams are kept at bay by a dreamcatcher. The art conveys a tenderness among the family members.

DISCUSS the kinds of things friends do to make each other feel important. What makes a friend special? How do we get along with friends? Sometimes friends might say and do things that hurt each other's feelings.

DO Print each student's name on an individual craft stick, and place all the sticks in a jar or box. Have each student pick a stick with the name of the friend who will receive a compliment. Cut out the compliments from one or two copies of the activity sheet and place them in a jar or box. Each child takes a turn pulling out a compliment and reads it to the friend named on the stick. As needed, help read the compliments.

RELATE the lesson to the children's daily lives by reviewing the importance of compliments in helping them feel good. Have children practice giving compliments to each other during circle time, noting that giving a compliment is a gift from the heart.

Secret Gift

LEARNING OBJECTIVES

Students will:

- gain a better understanding of empathy
- demonstrate how to use kind words and compliments

MATERIALS NEEDED

The book *When I Care About Others* by Cornelia Maude Spelman, "Secret Gift" activity sheet (page 124), scissors, pencils or pens, and crayons or markers

LESSON PLAN

READ *When I Care About Others*. A little bear explains that he cares about the feelings of others and that others care about him. The book includes some suggestions for promoting empathy.

> An optional book for teacher shared reading is *A Very Special Friend* by Dorothy Hoffman Levi. In search of a friend her own age, six-year-old Frannie meets Laura, who is deaf, and learns sign language from her.

DISCUSS   the kinds of things that friends do to show each other they care. One way to show someone you care is to use kind words that let the person know you understand how he or she feels. Brainstorm ways the kids can be more caring in the classroom.

DO the "Secret Gift" activity sheet. Have children cut out and create a compliment card to give to a friend in the classroom or school. Draw and color a picture on the front. Write a message inside to complete the phrase "I care about you because..."

RELATE the lesson to real life by allowing children to practice giving and receiving compliments during the exchange of their cards. How can they use what they have learned about being gracious?

If you wish to use this activity as part of a Valentine's Day celebration, have the children direct their compliment cards to family members or friends to express how much they care about them.

I Am Responsible

LEARNING OBJECTIVES

Students will:

- learn that responsibility and dependability are part of cooperation
- practice using cooperation skills

MATERIALS NEEDED

The book *The Little Red Hen* by Paul Galdone, "I Am Responsible" activity sheet (page 125), and pencils or pens

LESSON PLAN

READ   *The Little Red Hen*. The hen works very hard to do all the chores without any help from her three lazy animal friends.

> An optional text for teacher shared reading is *Babushka's Doll* by Patricia Polacco. In this tale, a selfish girl becomes "quite nice" after learning a valuable lesson from a doll that comes to life.

DISCUSS Define *responsibility (following through with what you have to do)* and *dependability (being someone that others can count on)*. Discuss how the little red hen felt when she thought she could count on her friends for help. What did her friends choose to do? What did the hen do about her friends? Ask children to think about what they do at home to help their families or at school to help each other. Are they going to be like the hen or her friends?

DO the "I Am Responsible" activity sheet. Each child draws a face showing how she or he feels when being helpful. Then have the kids draw pictures of times they showed responsibility.

RELATE how being helpful is also part of cooperation. Children show responsibility when they cooperate and help one another. Collect the completed activity sheets and make a classroom book or bulletin board titled "We Are Responsible."

Responsibility Zones

LEARNING OBJECTIVES

Students will:

- learn about responsibility and how to do their fair share
- discover that responsibility also includes kindness

MATERIALS NEEDED

The book *Heartprints* by P. K. Hallinan, "Responsibility Zones" activity sheet (page 126), and pencils or pens

LESSON PLAN

READ *Heartprints*. The illustrations and rhyming text show how we can brighten the world with acts of kindness and caring.

An optional book for teacher shared reading is *Mike Mulligan and His Steam Shovel* by Virginia Lee Burton. Mike makes a promise and keeps it, even though his shovel gets stuck.

DISCUSS Involve the class in brainstorming a list of the different ways to help at home, at school, or in the community. Use the story you read as a starting point for the brainstorming.

DO the "Responsibility Zones" activity sheet. Students decide if each action is showing responsibility. Then they draw or write about their favorite job and their least favorite job.

RELATE the activity to life at home and school by asking children to share their favorite and least favorite jobs in each place. How many had the same ideas? Sometimes being responsible isn't going to be fun. What can they do to make their least favorite jobs more enjoyable? Discuss the importance of getting things done even when the work may not be much fun.

Team Puzzles

LEARNING OBJECTIVES

Students will:

- learn to cooperate and solve problems in teams
- practice sharing and taking turns

MATERIALS NEEDED

The book *The Doorbell Rang* by Pat Hutchins, "Team Puzzles" activity sheet (page 127), scissors, envelopes, and prepared snacks in cups

LESSON PLAN

READ *The Doorbell Rang*. Mom's cookies prove irresistible not only to her offspring but also to their many friends. As the treats dwindle at an alarming rate with each new arrival, the kids learn cooperation and math concepts.

An optional text for teacher shared reading is *The F Team* by Anne Laurel Carter. With figure skates on their feet and determination in their hearts, Fanny and her friends set out to practice hockey to get better at the game.

DISCUSS how the children in the story had to cooperate so everyone got a cookie. What did they have to do every time a new person arrived? Was that fair? What happened in the end?

DO the "Team Puzzles" activity. Prior to class, cut apart the puzzle pieces (both puzzles) from one activity sheet. Place the pieces of both puzzles into an envelope. Prepare an envelope for each small group. Divide the class into small groups. Using the pieces from one envelope, the members of the group work together to put together the two puzzles. Don't tell the groups there are two puzzles in the envelope unless they cannot figure out how to assemble the puzzles.

RELATE how working on the puzzles is like a lot of things in life—it required cooperation. What was hard about working in the group and what was easy? How long did it take to figure out there were two puzzles? How did the group decide the best way to figure out the puzzles? Did everyone get a chance to help? Why or why not?

Close the activity by having the children practice sharing. Give each small group a cup with the same amount of crackers or other treat. Ask them to divide the snack equally among the members of the group. Ask the group what problems might be encountered while dividing the snack. How can the problems be solved? Celebrate by eating the treat. Reflect on how we get along best when we share and cooperate.

School of Sharing Fish

LEARNING OBJECTIVES

Students will:

- learn to appreciate sharing and generosity
- demonstrate their sharing skills

MATERIALS NEEDED

The book *The Rainbow Fish* by Marcus Pfister and translated by J. Alison James, "School of Sharing Fish" activity sheet (page 128), pencils or pens, markers or crayons, colored tissue paper or sequins or metallic stickers, scissors, and glue

LESSON PLAN

READ   *The Rainbow Fish*. Rainbow Fish refuses to share his beautiful scales. When his greed leaves him without friends, the lonely fish seeks advice from the wise octopus, who tells him that sharing is a better way to make friends.

An optional book for teacher shared reading is *It's Mine!* by Leo Lionni. A toad saves three young frogs from a flood and endless bickering.

DISCUSS   Why did Rainbow Fish have such a hard time sharing? What happened when Rainbow Fish chose not to share? How did Rainbow Fish feel when his friends didn't play with him? What did he learn about sharing?

DO   the "School of Sharing Fish" activity sheet. Have students color and cut out the fish. Glue scales to the fish by using shiny sequins or metallic stickers or tissue paper squares. Create a bulletin board to display the school of sharing fish.

RELATE   the story you read to real-life situations. Talk about how Rainbow Fish lost all his friends by being selfish. When he shared with the other fish, he made friends. What does the story tell the students about their behavior at school?

Apology Accepted

LEARNING OBJECTIVES

Students will:

- learn about taking responsibility for their actions
- understand how important it is to apologize and forgive

MATERIALS NEEDED

The book *Lilly's Purple Plastic Purse* by Kevin Henkes, "Apology Accepted" activity sheet (page 129), and pencils or pens

LESSON PLAN

READ   *Lilly's Purple Plastic Purse*. Lilly loves everything about school, especially her teacher, Mr. Slinger—until he takes away her musical purse because she can't stop playing with it in class. This book teaches about listening, patience, apologies, and forgiveness.

An optional text for teacher shared reading is *Roses Are Pink, Your Feet Really Stink* by Diane de Groat. Gilbert writes not-so-nice Valentine poems for two rude classmates, and he signs *their names* to the cards.

DISCUSS   Why was Lilly's purse taken away? How did that make Lilly feel? What did Lilly choose to do? Did Lilly use kind words to share how she felt? What happened at the end of the school day? How did Lilly feel when she got home? What did she do? What choice did Lilly make at the end of the story?

DO   the "Apology Accepted" activity sheet. Encourage children to think of a time when they thought an apology was needed. Ask them to draw a picture to show what happened. If they have difficulty sharing personal stories, they may use the story you read earlier.

RELATE   the importance of being responsible for our own actions to what can happen when we choose not to be responsible. Explain to the children that no one is perfect. When we make mistakes, apologies and forgiveness are an important part of getting along.

Working Together

LEARNING OBJECTIVES

Students will:

- learn the steps for working together
- participate in team building

MATERIALS NEEDED

The book *Working Together* by Pam Scheunemann, 10 pieces of cardboard or colored construction paper, and tape

LESSON PLAN

READ *Working Together*. Students will learn the important steps of working together to get things done and to get along.

An optional text for teacher shared reading is *The Ant and the Grasshopper*, by Aesop and retold by Amy Lowry Poole. A colony of industrious ants prepare for the approaching winter while a grasshopper makes no plans for the coming cold weather.

DISCUSS Review the steps of cooperation from the book. Emphasize the need for listening, sharing, taking turns, and helping each other.

DO a teamwork activity by playing Crossover. Tape cardboard or construction paper rectangles end-to-end on the floor. Have kids line up at both ends. At the same time, the first person in each line must walk on the paper and cross to the other end without stepping off the "bridge" and falling into the "water." Provide ground rules so children know they have to work together in order to pass each other on the bridge. Everyone gets a chance to cross the bridge. What creative ways can the kids find to work together?

RELATE the difficulties of crossing the bridge without falling into the water to working in teams. Review how students did working together. What was the best part and the hardest part of this activity? How did they help each other get the job done?

Trust Is Golden

LEARNING OBJECTIVES

Students will:

- learn what it means to trust someone
- practice trusting someone

MATERIALS NEEDED

The book *Jack and the Beanstalk* as retold by Carol Ottolenghi and blindfolds

LESSON PLAN

READ *Jack and the Beanstalk*. Jack wants to help his poor mother, but when he decides to sell the family cow for a handful of magic beans, he finds himself in a giant-sized mess.

An optional story for teacher shared reading is *The Three Little Pigs* as retold by Patricia Seibert. Each pig has built a house, but which one will survive the big, bad wolf? Would teamwork have helped?

DISCUSS the meaning of *trust*. What did Jack's mother ask him to do? Did he follow those directions? Did Jack make the right choices? Talk about how important it is to follow through when someone is expecting something of us. Ask students to share situations where trust is important.

DO Have kids work in small groups to retell the story of Jack with an ending that shows he made better choices by following his mother's directions.

RELATE the activity to the need for students and friends to trust and be trusted. Have students share their new endings to the story and talk about what they learned about trust.

Cooperation—Teaming Up for Success Quiz

Use the quiz activity sheet (page 130) to review and assess what the students learned this month. *(Answers: 1-T, 2-F, 3-T, 4-F, 5-T, 6-caring, 7-Team, 8-trust, 9-home, school)*

SAFE & CARING
VOCABULARY BUILDER

Word Find

H	O	N	E	S	T	F	P
J	A	H	U	L	N	T	R
R	E	W	S	N	A	E	L
S	E	C	R	E	T	A	U
O	A	T	F	E	R	M	F
R	S	E	G	Y	O	R	P
R	K	M	D	O	P	I	L
Y	Q	L	E	I	M	C	E
L	C	F	I	N	I	S	H

Circle these words in the Word Find puzzle.
(Hint: Words can run up, down, forward, backward, or diagonally.)

Key Words:
ASK
SORRY
FINISH
SECRET
TEAM

Challenge Words:
ANSWER
HONEST
IDEAS
IMPORTANT
HELPFUL

Fill in the blanks with vowels to complete the words

_nsw_r   t_ _m   h_n_st

_d_ _s   s_cr_t   f_n_sh

we are
a safe
& caring
SCHOOL.

THAT'S WHAT I LIKE ABOUT YOU

I like you.	You are nice.	You are happy.	You are a good friend.
You make me laugh.	You are caring.	You are cool.	You have a nice smile.
I like the way you play.	I'm glad you are in my class.	You are smart.	You are a good artist.
I like playing with you.	I'm glad we are friends.	I like the way you share.	You make me smile.
You are a good helper.	You are a good listener.	You are the best.	You are fun to know.
I like the way you talk.	You are a good reader.	You are friendly.	You are good at sports.

From *Activities for Building Character and Social-Emotional Learning Grades 1–2* by Katia S. Petersen, Ph.D., copyright © 2012. Free Spirit Publishing Inc., Minneapolis, MN; 800-735-7323; www.freespirit.com. This page may be reproduced for individual, classroom, and small group work only. For all other uses, contact www.freespirit.com/company/permissions.cfm.

SAFE & CARING SCHOOLS®

SKILLS FOR SCHOOL. SKILLS FOR LIFE.

SECRET GIFT

To: From:

A Gift from the Heart

I care about you because...

I am RESPONSIBLE

Define **responsible**: _____

_____

_____

Draw a face to show how you feel when you are being helpful.

Then draw a picture of a time when you were being responsible and helpful.

we are a safe & caring school.

FEBRUARY

RESPONSIBILITY ZONES

Write the numbers of these "Actions" in the correct box to show which actions are responsible and which are not.

Responsible			Not Responsible

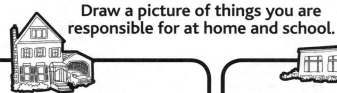

1) Help set the table
2) Clean my room
3) Forget to do my homework
4) Brush my teeth

5) Did not feed my pet
6) Use my quiet voice
7) Share my toys
8) Ran through the halls at school

Draw a picture of things you are responsible for at home and school.

Home

School

Answer these questions.

My favorite job is _____

_____

_____

My least favorite job is _____

_____

_____

we aRe a saFe & CaRiNG SCHOOL.

TEaM PUZZLES

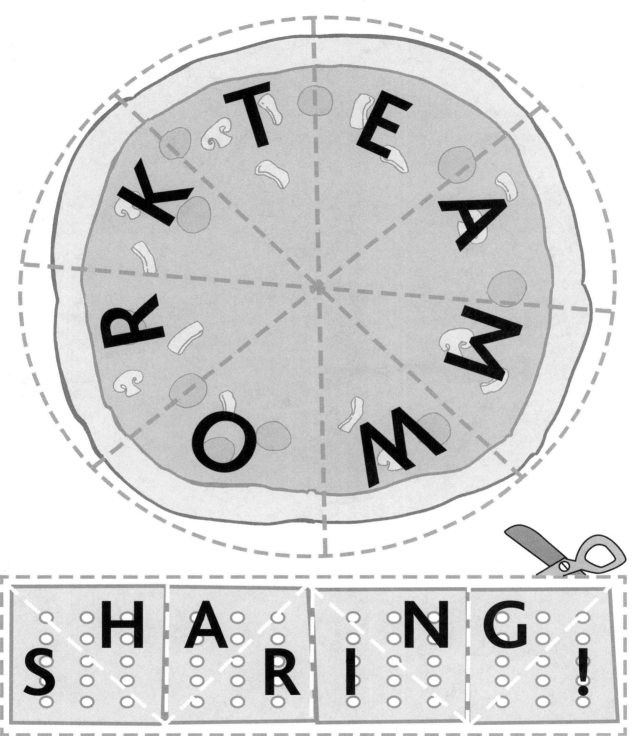

SCHOOL OF SHARING FISH

we are
a safe
& caring
SCHOOL.

APOLOGY ACCEPTED

Draw

Draw a picture of a time when you needed to apologize.

When we apologize it helps us get along.

How did you feel before and after the apology?

WE ARE A SAFE & CARING SCHOOL.

COOPERATION—TEAMING UP FOR SUCCESS QUIZ

True or False (circle the correct answer)

1) Teamwork helps get things done. .... **True / False**

2) Sharing is not important as long as work gets done. .... **True / False**

3) I am responsible when I help my team. .... **True / False**

4) It is okay to be bossy when I am on a team. .... **True / False**

5) I show respect when I am wrong by saying,

"I'm sorry." .... **True / False**

Fill in the Blanks

Use these words to complete each sentence.

trust   caring   school   team   home

6) Teamwork makes our school safe and _____.

7) _____ members help one another.

8) Others _____ us when we are responsible.

9) We can be cooperative at _____ and at _____.

Draw or Write

10) When you were part of a team, what did you do together?

we are a safe & caring school.

MARCH

Getting Along with Others— Conflict Resolution

- **Active Listening**
- **Self-Control**

- **Respectful Communication**
- **Conflict Resolution**

Because conflict is a part of everyday life, students must recognize anger signals and learn how to deal with disagreements and differences in nonviolent ways. To do this, students must practice their listening skills and develop the ability to talk out problems and make wise choices.

MONTHLY OBJECTIVES

Students will:

- learn what conflict is, how it escalates, and how to respond to it assertively
- use the Stop, Think, Choose method to resolve conflict peacefully

TEACHING TIPS

- Give each student a few minutes of your undivided attention each day.
- Show students how to ask for attention in appropriate ways.
- Recognize children every time they make a good choice.
- Give each student a chance to succeed.

MARCH INTEGRATED ACTIVITIES

In addition to the specific lesson plans for this month, you can use these optional ideas to integrate and extend the Safe & Caring themes into daily routines and across the curricular areas.

LANGUAGE ARTS

- Read short stories about people who made a difference by promoting peace and peaceful conflict resolution.
- Ask students to write or draw pictures in their journals about conflict they managed to resolve in a peaceful way.
- Have students re-create a story by acting it out or using puppets. Ask them to give it their own peaceful ending.

LITERATURE

- Have students write their own short stories using words and pictures that show good listeners resolving conflict in positive ways.
- Read *The Biggest Pumpkin Ever* by Steven Kroll. Discuss the problem and the solution. As you read the story, pause and have students invent their own endings.
- Read *Don't Let the Pigeon Drive the Bus!* by Mo Willems. This book teaches about whining, demanding, and tantrums. What are alternatives to those negative behaviors?

SOCIAL STUDIES

- Define *conflict* and discuss the kinds of conflict students might engage in.
- What kind of conflict do students see at home, at school, or on television?
- Discuss ways people can resolve conflict peacefully.

ART

- Create collages or murals for the school that depict students working things out, listening, and showing respect.
- Use the "Caring Hearts" project (page 9) as a way to reward students for resolving conflicts in peaceful ways. Decorate the classroom or a bulletin board with a tree of hearts (see page 9) showing how many conflicts were resolved peacefully.

MUSIC

- Listen to songs from *Ideas, Thoughts and Feelings* or *Getting to Know Myself*, both by Hap Palmer (www.happalmer.com). Together, discuss the songs' messages about feelings.

MATH

- Read *Lemonade for Sale* by Stuart J. Murphy. Four children decide to sell lemonade to make money to fix their clubhouse. When competition shows up, they find a solution that helps both sides.

> *"We've seen a significant change in the attitude and the behavior of students. The students embrace the idea of a Safe & Caring School, and it's easier to discipline children when we have this philosophy."*
>
> **PRINCIPAL, TARBOX SCHOOL**

Safe & Caring Schools Vocabulary Builder

LEARNING OBJECTIVES

Students will:

- be introduced to vocabulary that supports getting along with one another and responsibly solving conflicts
- internalize the vocabulary as they use it throughout the month and year in real-life situations

MATERIALS NEEDED

"Safe & Caring Vocabulary Builder" activity sheet (page 138) and pencils

LESSON PLAN

Use the vocabulary activities to introduce the concepts and common language associated with this month's theme. Throughout the month, use the words in writing, spelling, storytelling, and dealing with conflict situations. Add the words to your word wall.

For the Word Find activity, choose to use the key words, challenge words, or both. Discuss what the words mean after completing the page. You may want students to work in pairs to help each other.

For the fill-in-the-blanks activity, have students work the math problems and use the answers to determine the vowels needed to complete the words. Define the words with the class *(agree, calm, turn, problem, mistake, bother, listen, stress, trouble)*

I Am a Good Listener

LEARNING OBJECTIVES

Students will:

- learn why it is important to listen
- practice the steps of active listening

MATERIALS NEEDED

The book *Listen, Buddy* by Helen Lester and "I Am a Good Listener" miniposter (page 139)

LESSON PLAN

READ *Listen, Buddy.* His ears are enormous, but listening is not the forte of a bunny named Buddy. His misinterpretations of his parents' requests make for the sort of silly confusion that youngsters love.

> An optional text for teacher shared reading is *The Surprise Party* by Pat Hutchins. One animal's message gets so mixed up as it is passed around that the only thing anyone knows for sure is that everybody has the wrong story.

DISCUSS Praise the children for doing a good job listening. Why is it important to listen? How does listening help us get things done right? What can happen between friends when someone doesn't listen? How do you feel when people choose not to listen to you?

DO Review the points of being a good listener by using the "I Am a Good Listener" miniposter. Have children share examples of when they were good listeners and when they had problems listening. Have the students use their miniposter as a frequent reminder of the skills of good listeners.

RELATE the theme of this lesson to life within the classroom. How can good listening skills help the children succeed in class? As an extended activity, play the telephone game during circle time. Whisper a special message to the child on your right. Have the child whisper the message to the person on his or her right, and so on until the message comes back to you. Review how well the message was passed from person to person. Discuss how easy it is to hear the wrong thing and get into arguments because of misunderstandings. Remind children they should practice good listening every day.

Good Listening

LEARNING OBJECTIVES

Students will:

- discover that skills of active listening are important in all they do
- demonstrate their active listening skills

MATERIALS NEEDED

The book *Sing, Sophie!* by Dayle Ann Dodds, "Good Listening" activity sheet (page 140), and crayons or markers

LESSON PLAN

READ *Sing, Sophie!* Sophie loves to sing, but no one wants to hear her song until a special situation calls for her talents. Sophie's cowgirl songs not only come in handy, but save the day as well.

> An optional text for teacher shared reading is *The Knight and the Dragon* by Tomie de Paola. An inexperienced knight and an equally inexperienced dragon prepare to meet each other in battle.

DISCUSS how active listening helps us get our work done, solve problems, and share what we are thinking and feeling with our friends. How did Sophie feel when no one was listening to her? What did Sophie continue to do throughout the story? What happened in the story that helped others listen to Sophie? Have the students ever tried to say something important and no one paid attention? How did they feel about it? What did they do?

DO the "Good Listening" activity sheet. Children decide if the situations show good listening skills. Color a smiley face if the answer is yes, a sad face if the answer is no.

RELATE the need to be a good listener to success in school. Discuss how much easier it is to get schoolwork done when you get the instructions the first time instead of having to repeatedly ask someone what to do. Review good listening skills in circle time and discuss ways to improve active listening every day.

Listening Journal

LEARNING OBJECTIVES

Students will:

- practice listening by paying attention to sounds around them
- keep a record of the sounds they hear

MATERIALS NEEDED

The book *The Listening Walk* by Paul Showers, "Listening Journal" activity sheet (page 141), and pencils or pens

LESSON PLAN

READ *The Listening Walk.* On a walk with her dad, a little girl learns how to pay attention to the many sounds of the neighborhood.

> An optional text for teacher shared reading is *Mog, the Forgetful Cat* by Judith Kerr. Mog's absent-minded ways get her into trouble.

DISCUSS how the girl's listening skills improved when she paid close attention. Have the children recall the sounds they hear in school, at home, when they go shopping, or in the neighborhood (*some possibilities are bells, laughing, talking, shoes walking, car engine, machines, tools, music*). What sounds get heard and what sounds get missed?

DO the "Listening Journal" activity sheet. For the next five days, ask the children to write one or more sounds they hear in school, at home, and in their neighborhoods. As an example, do together the "Day 1 School Sounds." The rest of the sheet will be a home activity, so send the sheet home and have the kids complete the chart by listening for sounds from their homes and neighborhoods, and remembering sounds heard at school that day. Remind the students to bring their completed listening journals back to class at the end of the five days.

RELATE how paying attention is important in school and in most everything kids do. Discuss the difference between hearing something and really listening. Help the children realize how important it is for them to pay attention.

After five days, compare the children's completed "Listening Journal" activity sheets. Which sounds were the same, which were different? Did anyone hear a sound that no one else heard?

My Anger Button

LEARNING OBJECTIVES

Children will:

- learn that people respond to conflict in different ways
- practice specific vocabulary related to conflict resolution

MATERIALS NEEDED

The book *Stop Picking on Me* by Pat Thomas, "My Anger Button" activity sheet (page 142), and crayons or markers

LESSON PLAN

READ *Stop Picking on Me.* When bullies pick on a boy at school, a classmate is afraid but decides he must do something. This book helps children accept the everyday fears and worries that result from bullying, and it suggests ways to resolve that kind of upsetting experience.

> An optional text for teacher shared reading is *Andrew's Angry Words* by Dorothea Lachner. Andrew's bad mood and swear words have a ripple effect on the people around him.

DISCUSS   the fact that everyone gets angry sometimes, but what makes us upset varies from person to person. These are our anger buttons. By understanding what upsets others, we can respond using kind words and actions. It is important to let our friends know what makes us feel angry so they know how to treat us with respect.

DO   the "My Anger Button" activity sheet. What makes one person angry does not necessarily make another person angry. Have the children respond to the different situations listed on the activity sheet and color the face corresponding to how they would feel. The activity may be done on an overhead projector as a class activity.

RELATE   the fact that how one responds to a given situation has a direct effect on the result of the situation. The reaction may diffuse or further ignite a tough situation. Check how the students responded to the situations on the activity sheet. Besides seeing how each person might respond to a situation, we need to pay attention to each other's feelings so we can show care and respect to others. Review the golden rule.

A Better Way to Say It

LEARNING OBJECTIVES

Students will:

- recognize that unkind words can hurt others' feelings
- learn to choose how to say things in a respectful way

MATERIALS NEEDED

The book *I Want It* by Elizabeth Crary, "A Better Way to Say It" activity sheet (page 143), pencils or pens, and puppets

LESSON PLAN

READ   *I Want It.* With this book children have the opportunity to practice problem-solving skills and making choices in realistic situations.

> An optional text for teacher shared reading is *Eggbert, the Slightly Cracked Egg* by Tom Ross. The other eggs in the refrigerator admire Eggbert's remarkable paintings—until they discover that he has a slight crack. Because of his defect, he is banished from his home.

DISCUSS   the different behaviors of the children in the book. Talk about the difference between hurtful and respectful words. Ask children how they feel when someone uses unkind words with them. How could those unkind words be replaced with something more positive that makes both kids feel better?

DO   the "A Better Way to Say It" activity sheet. For beginning readers, you may want to read each statement from the "Hurtful Words" column. Have children use puppets to demonstrate an alternative to the hurtful words. What would be the respectful way to say it? This activity may be done with the entire class by making an overhead transparency of the activity sheet.

RELATE   the lesson to real life by having the children brainstorm respectful actions and words they can use in their classroom and throughout the school. Create a "kind words" box. Copy and place the Caring Hearts from page 54 into the box. Use them as handy rewards to give students each time they use respectful words and actions.

Conflict Cartoons

LEARNING OBJECTIVES

Students will:

- explore strategies to deal with conflict in positive ways
- learn about copycats

MATERIALS NEEDED

The book *Stephanie's Ponytail* by Robert Munsch, "Conflict Cartoons" activity sheet (page 144), pencils or pens, and crayons or markers

LESSON PLAN

READ *Stephanie's Ponytail*. A little girl chooses to wear unique hairdos each day. As her schoolmates copy her style, her anger grows until she threatens to shave her head to stop the copycats.

> An optional text for teacher shared reading is *I Want to Play* by Elizabeth Crary. Danny is tired of playing alone. He wants to join the other kids. The reader gets to choose what Danny will do to solve his problem.

DISCUSS What was the problem in the story? How did Stephanie feel about the way she was treated in class? How did the other children feel about Stephanie? Who helped Stephanie find a good solution to the problem? What choice did Stephanie make by the end of the story?

DO the "Conflict Cartoons" activity sheet. Have the children create a cartoon strip to demonstrate a positive way to solve a conflict.

RELATE the Stop, Think, Choose strategy (page 42) to real-life issues the children are experiencing. How have they been able to resolve conflicts in positive ways? Review the children's cartoons from the activity sheet. Can they think of other ways to solve problems? Did they use the Stop, Think, Choose strategy?

What's the Problem?

LEARNING OBJECTIVES

Students will:

- learn how to find solutions to problems that are acceptable to both parties
- practice their conflict resolution skills (Stop, Think, Choose)

MATERIALS NEEDED

The book *The Owl and the Woodpecker* by Brian Wildsmith, "What's the Problem?" activity sheet (page 145), and pencils or pens

LESSON PLAN

READ *The Owl and the Woodpecker*. The Woodpecker sleeps all night and works all day. His neighbor, Owl, works all night and sleeps all day. Because of this, they argue so much that it upsets all the other animals.

DISCUSS why the owl was so upset with the woodpecker. How did Woodpecker feel when Owl was so angry? What solution did Owl and Woodpecker use to solve their problem? Ask the children if they ever had an argument with a friend because their friend was not being considerate. How did they feel about it, and what did they choose to do?

DO the "What's the Problem?" activity sheet. If you read *The Owl and the Woodpecker*, use the story as the basis for identifying and solving a problem using the Stop, Think, Choose steps. If you haven't read the book, give the students a problem that frequently comes up at school.

RELATE the lesson to the daily activities of the students by reiterating the importance of using the Stop, Think, Choose steps when they are upset. Remind children that if they have a hard time solving a problem on their own, they should ask for help from someone they know and trust.

Safe & Caring Ways to Solve Problems

LEARNING OBJECTIVES

Students will:

- identify positive ways to resolve conflicts
- realize they can choose how they respond to conflict

MATERIALS NEEDED

The book *Katharine's Doll* by Elizabeth Winthrop, "Safe & Caring Ways to Solve Problems" activity sheet (page 146), and crayons or markers

LESSON PLAN

READ   *Katharine's Doll*. Two girls are best friends until one of them gets a new doll. After arguing over the doll, the girls realize their friendship is much more important than a toy.

An optional text for teacher shared reading is *Tristan's Temper Tantrum* by Caroline Formby. Awakening from a thousand year slumber, baby Tristan finds that nobody wants to play with a bad-tempered volcano.

DISCUSS   Why did the girls have an argument? How did the girls feel about each other? What did the girls choose to do? Brainstorm with the children a list of things people usually do when they have arguments and disagreements. Discuss good choices and bad choices people make when they are angry. Remind the class they have the power to choose how to respond to conflict.

DO   the "Safe & Caring Ways to Solve Problems" activity sheet. Have the children indicate whether the responses to problems are good or bad choices by coloring in the appropriate face. You may need to read the choices to beginning readers, and they can respond with a thumbs-up (good choice) or thumbs-down (bad choice).

RELATE   the importance of choosing positive ways for solving problems to actual situations at school. Remind the children that each day you want them to try their best to make good choices. Tell them that because they are all friends, they should help each other remember to get along.

Do the Right Thing

LEARNING OBJECTIVES

Students will:

- learn to control the things they say and do
- practice making the right choices

MATERIALS NEEDED

The book *Noisy Nora* by Rosemary Wells, "Do the Right Thing" activity sheet (page 147), and pencils or pens

LESSON PLAN

READ   *Noisy Nora*. A mouse chooses to make plenty of noise when little brother and big sister take up all of Mom and Dad's time.

An optional text for teacher shared reading is *Sheila Rae's Peppermint Stick* by Kevin Henkes. The familiar theme of sibling rivalry surfaces between the heroine and her younger sister, Louise.

DISCUSS   the right and wrong ways to get attention. Review the story. Explain what it means to be "the boss of the things we say and do." Review the steps of Stop, Think, Choose (page 42).

DO   the "Do the Right Thing" activity sheet. The students consider the "right" way to solve four situations. This activity can be done on the overhead projector with the entire class.

RELATE   the lesson to the children's daily activities in the classroom or on the playground. How can practicing the use of kind words, keeping hands and feet to themselves, using inside voices, and helping friends in need, make a better environment in which to learn and play?

Getting Along with Others— Conflict Resolution Quiz

Use the quiz activity sheet (page 148) to review and assess what the students learned this month. *(Answers: 1-T, 2-F, 3-T, 4-T, 5-T, 6-Friends, 7-listening, problems, 8-choice, 9-trust)*

SAFE & CARING VOCABULARY BUILDER

Word Find

A	G	R	E	E	S	P	C
K	U	X	Y	R	R	R	O	W
H	O	P	L	Z	N	O	G
S	Z	O	R	F	E	S	K
U	C	A	L	M	Y	H	I
P	N	I	S	U	R	A	R
M	C	R	E	U	G	R	A
T	R	O	U	B	L	E	C
G	E	V	A	T	K	O	J

Circle these words in the Word Find puzzle.
(Hint: Words can run up, down, forward, backward, or diagonally.)

Key Words:
CALM
PUSH
LOOK
SHARE
TURN

Challenge Words:
AGREE
ARGUE
TROUBLE
WORRY
CONFLICT

Solve the math problems and use the number code to finish the words.

Number Code: 1=a   2=e   3=i   4=o   5=u

3 – 2 = __ = __gree   2 + 2 = __ = pr__blem   (7 + 2) – 6 = __ = l__sten

4 – 3 = __ = c__lm   5 – 4 = __ = mist__ke   (8 + 4) – 10 = __ = str__ss

15 – 10 = __ = t__rn   1 + 3 = __ = b__ther   3 + 1 = __ = tr__uble

we are
a safe
& caring
school.

I am a GOOD LISTENER

- I sit quietly.

- I look at the person who is speaking.

- I don't interrupt.

- I wait for my turn to talk.

- I ask questions.

we aRe a safe & CaRiNG SCHOOL.

GOOD LISTENING

Which of these are good listening habits?

your choice

Yes   No

Paying attention when someone is talking.

Looking at the person who is speaking.

Deciding not to ask questions when I don't understand.

Not caring how the speaker feels.

Sitting quietly and not interrupting.

Being impatient and not waiting for my turn to speak.

Being polite.

we are a safe & caring school.

LISTENING JOURNAL

Home Sounds

Neighborhood Sounds

School Sounds

	Home Sounds	Neighborhood Sounds	School Sounds
Day 1			
Day 2			
Day 3			
Day 4			
Day 5			

we are a safe & caring school.

MY ANGER BUTTON

For each situation, color the face that shows how you would feel.

	Happy	Sad	Mad	Scared
When I'm teased, I feel...				
When someone is being bossy, I feel...				
When my friends do not want to share, I feel...				
When I'm not invited to a birthday party, I feel...				
When someone takes my things without asking, I feel...				
When my brother or sister gets all the attention, I feel...				
When my friend moves away, I feel...				
When someone calls me a name, I feel...				
When I make mistakes, I feel...				

we are a safe & CARING SCHOOL.

A BETTER WAY TO SAY IT

Hurtful Words	Respectful Words
 Stop it!	
Go away! I don't want to play with you!	
I don't like you!	
Give me that!	
You're not my friend anymore!	

CONFLICT CARTOONS

Create a cartoon about the best way to solve conflicts. Share it with your friends.

WE ARE a SaFe & CARING SCHOOL.

WHAT'S THE PROBLEM?

Solve the problem with Stop, Think, Choose.

What is the problem?

What can be done about it?

Make the best choice!

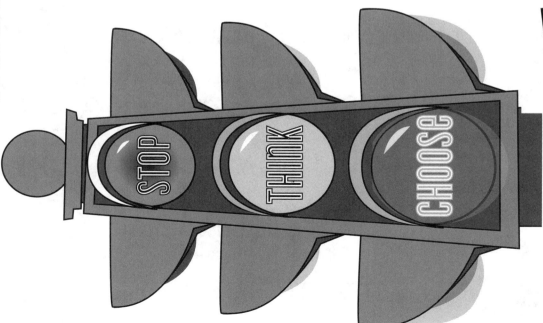

we are a safe & caring school.

MARCH

Safe & Caring
Ways to Solve Problems

When there's a problem, I choose to...

	Good Choice	Bad Choice

...talk to a friend.

...kick my brother, sister, or pet.

...ride my bike around the block.

...call someone a bad name.

...talk to a grown-up I trust.

...go to my room until I calm down.

...write a story or draw a picture.

...scream and throw a tantrum.

...listen to music

...STOP, THINK, CHOOSE.

we are a safe & caring school.

DO THE RIGHT THING

How would you use Stop, Think, Choose to solve these problems?

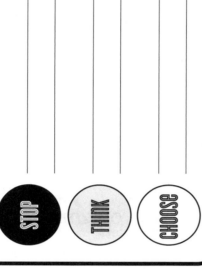

Other kids always try to pull Jamie's ponytail.

STOP THINK CHOOSE

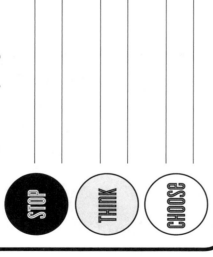

James always cuts in line at lunch.

STOP THINK CHOOSE

Two classmates both want the same ball at recess.

STOP THINK CHOOSE

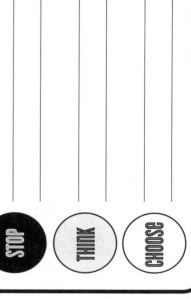

You see Heather steal something at the store.

STOP THINK CHOOSE

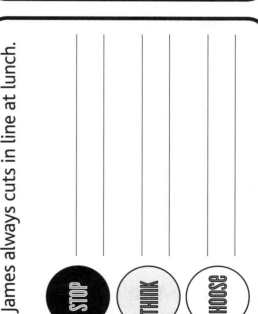

When I do the right thing I feel...

Circle one.

MARCH

we aRe
a saFe
& CaRiNG
SCHOOL.

GETTING ALONG WITH OTHERS— CONFLICT RESOLUTION QUIZ

True or False (circle the correct answer)

1) Conflict is a part of life. .... True / False

2) I don't have to be respectful when someone
   isn't respectful to me. .... True / False

3) Being a good listener helps me get
   along with others. .... True / False

4) I should listen to others even if they
   don't listen to me. .... True / False

5) There are steps I can follow to solve problems. .... True / False

Fill in the Blanks

Use these words to complete the sentences:

choices   problems   trust   friends   listening

6) _____ talk to each other with respect.

7) By _____ carefully, we can solve _____.

8) We can make the right _____ when we Stop,
   Think, Choose.

9) Ask a grown-up you know and _____ for help.

Draw or Write

10) Describe how you solved a problem by listening carefully
    and using Stop, Think, Choose.

we are a safe & caring school.

APRIL
The Power to Choose

- **Making Choices**
- **Consequences**

- **Fairness**

Making good choices is a lifelong skill, and taking responsibility for one's choices is an essential character trait for today's children and youth. Our students are challenged, tempted, and bullied. They have more opportunities to get into trouble than ever before. Children need to be taught to use the power of their minds in positive ways to make the appropriate choices in their lives.

MONTHLY OBJECTIVES
Students will:

- learn what it means to be responsible for their own actions
- practice treating people with fairness and respect

TEACHING TIPS

- Help children understand that making good choices is related to controlling the anger that results from stress, frustration, feeling rejected, and isolation.
- Teach students how to manage anger and channel its energy in useful and productive ways.
- Instill in children the understanding that they have the power to choose to respond to anger and conflict in constructive ways.
- Practice positive reinforcement to model how to manage anger and make better choices.

APRIL INTEGRATED ACTIVITIES

In addition to the specific lesson plans for this month, you can use these optional ideas to integrate and extend the Safe & Caring themes into daily routines and across the curricular areas.

LANGUAGE ARTS

- Have students write a story about a time they made a good choice.
- Students can write short stories or poems to relate their feelings about choices and consequences.

LITERATURE

- Have students choose books from the library dealing with the concepts of fairness, justice, choices, and consequences. In small groups, students can compare the characters in their books to explore how each one behaved in a given situation.
- Read *Chester's Way* by Kevin Henkes. Lilly moves into the neighborhood and has her own way of doing things. Chester and Wilson don't know what to make of her until the day she helps them. After that, Chester and Wilson look at Lilly differently and discover that the three of them have many things in common. They realize that there are different ways of doing things and that different is just fine.
- Read *Lizard's Song* by George Shannon. When Bear wants something, he takes it, and he wants Lizard's song. Discuss the importance of being patient and how it helps us make better choices and get along with our friends.
- Read *Strega Nona* by Tomie dePaola. Big Anthony gets in trouble when he chooses not to listen to Strega Nona's warning about touching her magic pasta pot. Talk about using your power to make the right choices.

SOCIAL STUDIES

- Read *The Other Side* by Jacqueline Woodson. This is a story of friendship across a racial divide. Talk about fairness and courage. Ask a student to assume the role of one of the girls and role-play her character and the conflicts with the class, expressing her feelings and emotions in making choices related to friendship.

ART

- Have students create a "Wall of Respect" by drawing pictures depicting one of the character traits from this month's theme.
- Create a classroom book called "Making Good Choices" that depicts situations kids may face in daily life at school.

MUSIC

- Listen to songs about friendship and working together on *Free to Be . . . You and Me* (www .freetobefoundation.org) or on CDs by the Laurie Berkner Band (www.laurieberkner.com). Discuss the songs' messages.

MATH

- Read *Henry the Fourth* by Stuart J. Murphy. With this story children learn about sequential numbers as well as fairness. Four pets are entered in a backyard dog show and are identified as first, second, third, and fourth. Following this order, they each do a trick as planned, except for Henry, the last dog to be introduced.

Safe & Caring Schools Vocabulary Builder

LEARNING OBJECTIVES

Students will:

- be introduced to vocabulary that supports making good choices for a safe and caring classroom, and for life

- internalize the vocabulary as they use it throughout the month and year in real-life situations

MATERIALS NEEDED

"Safe & Caring Vocabulary Builder" activity sheet (page 157) and pencils

LESSON PLAN

Use the vocabulary activities to introduce the concepts and common language associated with this month's theme. Throughout the month, use the words in writing, spelling, storytelling, and dealing with conflict situations. Add the words to your word wall.

For the Word Find activity, choose to use the key words, challenge words, or both. Discuss what the words mean after completing the page. You may want students to work in pairs to help each other.

For the fill-in-the-blanks activity, have students fill in the blanks using words from the Word Find activity *(power, truth, talk, fair, positive)*

My Choices

LEARNING OBJECTIVES

Students will:

- realize that they make both good and bad choices during the week

- learn that they must deal with the consequences of their choices

MATERIALS NEEDED

The book *My Big Lie* by Bill Cosby, "My Choices" activity sheet (page 158), and pencils or pens

LESSON PLAN

READ *My Big Lie*. Little Bill gets in big trouble when he tells a lie to explain why he came home late for dinner.

> An optional text for teacher shared reading is *We Can Get Along: A Child's Book of Choices* by Lauren Murphy Payne. The book's theme is that individuals choose how to behave. Everyone can share, respect others, think before speaking, work out problems, and enjoy many types of friends.

DISCUSS Ask students to think of the kinds of choices they make every day. Emphasize that sometimes we make good choices, and sometimes we make poor choices. What choice did Bill make to explain his being late? Was it the right choice? Help children understand there are consequences for every choice, for example, if I choose to hit, my friend will not play with me; or, if I don't listen, I won't know what to do.

DO the "My Choices" activity sheet. At the end of each day for a week, have students write the good choices and the poor choices they made under the appropriate happy or sad face.

RELATE After the students write their daily choices on the activity sheets, relate the choices they made to how they feel and to the impact the choices may have had on their friends. Remind students that it takes practice to learn how to make good choices, which is why you will help them practice every day.

Positive Choice!

LEARNING OBJECTIVES

Students will:

- understand they are responsible for their own actions
- learn they can choose how to respond when they are treated unfairly

MATERIALS NEEDED

The book *Shrinking Violet* by Cari Best, "Positive Choice!" activity sheet (page 159), pencils or pens, and crayons or markers

LESSON PLAN

READ *Shrinking Violet.* Violet is very shy and easily embarrassed, especially when other children tease her. She finally comes out of her shell when she is cast in a play and saves the production from disaster.

> An optional text for teacher shared reading is *The Princess and the Dragon* by Audrey Wood. The princess has terrible behavior. She meets a dragon that wants to be a princess, and the fun begins when they switch places.

DISCUSS   How was Violet treated in the story? How did she feel about being treated that way? What did Violet choose to do with her feelings? How did Violet choose to save the day? Remind students that we have the power to choose the way we respond to how people treat us. Even when we feel angry, sad, or frustrated, we still have choices for what to do with our feelings.

DO   the "Positive Choice!" activity sheet. Ask children to draw a picture story of a time they made a good choice in a tough situation. As they work, talk about how we are responsible for our own actions. Use examples they relate to, such as if someone chooses to call me a name, I can choose to ignore her, walk away, say "stop", or ask for help.

RELATE   making good choices to the real-life choices the kids make at school every day. Have the children share their picture stories and other examples of being faced with choices. How does choosing wisely make the day more pleasant in school? What happens when poor choices are made? (Give examples of choices and consequences.) You may want to use the activity sheets to create a classroom book titled, "Our Choices."

What Could Happen?

LEARNING OBJECTIVES

Students will:

- discover there are always consequences for the choices they make
- experience positive consequences instead of negative ones by changing behavior and making good choices

MATERIALS NEEDED

The book *Me First* by Helen Lester, "What Could Happen?" activity sheet (page 160), and pencils or pens

LESSON PLAN

READ   *Me First.* Pinkerton the Pig is pushy so he can be the first one on the bus, the first one in the water, and the first one down the slide. He finally learns that first is not always best.

> An optional text for teacher shared reading is *I Can't Wait* by Elizabeth Crary. A little boy thinks of many different things to do while waiting to take his turn.

DISCUSS   Does Pinkerton think about others in his rush to be first? What do the other children think of Pinkerton? What happens to him because of his "me first" attitude? Help children understand the direct connection between feelings, actions, and consequences: I feel angry (feeling); I choose to hit (action); I get in trouble (consequence). What did Pinkerton feel and choose to do? What were the consequences of his actions?

DO   the "What Could Happen?" activity sheet. Students are given a scenario and two choices. They must decide what the consequences are for each choice and make the best decision of what to do. This activity may be done on the overhead as a class activity.

RELATE   the idea of choices and consequences to everyday life for your students. Remind students that if they choose not to think about how others will be affected by their actions, they stand to lose the respect of others, and their friends, in the process. Help your students think beyond immediate effects of certain choices to explore the long-term consequences.

Good Friends, Tough Choices

LEARNING OBJECTIVES

Students will:

- understand the difference between asking for help and tattling
- use a simple question that helps them decide when to ask for help

MATERIALS NEEDED

The book *A Weekend with Wendell* by Kevin Henkes, "Telling or Tattling?" activity sheet (page 161), and pencils or pens

LESSON PLAN

READ A Weekend with Wendell. Sophie and her parents count the hours until Wendell's weekend visit is over as he breaks all the rules and forgets his manners.

> An optional text for teacher shared reading is *The Gigantic Turnip* by Aleksei Tolstoy and Niamh Sharkey. An old man and woman and all of the animals try to uproot a gigantic turnip. In the end, a tiny mouse makes a big difference so everyone can enjoy a hearty turnip supper.

DISCUSS Why did Sophie and her parents have such difficulty dealing with Wendell? Discuss the difference between telling *(trying to help yourself or someone else from getting into trouble)* and tattling *(trying to get someone into trouble)*. Sometimes we may have difficulty knowing what to do when there is trouble. Sometimes it is best to not say anything when it is tattling. But remember that asking for help is not the same as tattling.

DO the "Telling or Tattling?" activity sheet. Children respond to different situations and decide if they are telling or tattling, and why. This activity can be done on the overhead projector as a class activity.

RELATE this lesson to life at school. Which of the situations on the activity sheet could happen at school? How do students know if it is a situation that calls for help from an adult? What question do they need to ask themselves before reporting something? *(Is it getting someone out of or into trouble?)*

Author for a Day

LEARNING OBJECTIVES

Students will:

- learn to find positive solutions to problems
- practice their creative thinking and writing skills

MATERIALS NEEDED

The book *Lilly's Big Day* by Kevin Henkes, "Author for a Day" activity sheet (page 162), and pencils or pens

LESSON PLAN

READ Lilly's Big Day. Lilly's favorite teacher is getting married, and Lilly plans on being the flower girl. When a niece gets chosen instead, Lilly is sad and mad.

> An optional text for teacher shared reading is *Enemy Pie* by Derek Munson. A boy is being pushed around by a new kid on the block until his dad shows him how to turn an enemy into a friend.

DISCUSS Why did Lilly think she was going to be the flower girl? Who got the position instead? What did Mr. Slinger do to help the situation? How did Lilly handle the new role she was given? How did it all end? How did Lilly solve her problem in a creative and positive way?

DO the "Author for a Day" activity sheet. Children may write a story about a time they had to make a tough decision, or they may retell the story of Lilly in their own words.

RELATE Use the students' stories to talk more about making tough decisions. Have volunteers sit in a special "author" chair to share their stories. Create an "Author for a Day" sign and post it on the chair. Discuss what it means to be creative in solving problems. What examples can the students give on finding positive ways to handle conflict?

Give and Take

LEARNING OBJECTIVES

Students will:

- learn the art of negotiation and compromise (give and take) to resolve conflicts
- practice negotiation skills

MATERIALS NEEDED

The book *Click, Clack, Moo: Cows That Type* by Doreen Cronin, "Give and Take" activity sheet (page 163), and pencils or pens

LESSON PLAN

READ   *Click, Clack, Moo: Cows That Type*. Farmer Brown's cows find an old typewriter and begin typing their complaints. The book illustrates the power of peaceful protest and the satisfaction of cooperative give and take.

An optional text for teacher shared reading is *The Knight and the Dragon* by Tomie dePaola. A rookie knight and an equally inexperienced dragon must prepare for battle, but they find a way to "give and take" so they are both happy.

DISCUSS   Define the phrase *give and take (negotiate and compromise)* and discuss why it is important to learn how to do both. How did the farmer and his animals come to a fair solution? What evidence is there that they did give and take?

DO   the "Give and Take" activity sheet. Students are given four problem situations where they come up with solutions. In determining what to say, they need to consider how the characters can give and take.

RELATE   the importance of giving and taking in situations that arise in the school day. Sample situations to consider might include these: two kids want the same toy or ball at recess; two kids want to read the same book for a report; or two kids each want the class to play a different game. If you are using the "Caring Hearts" program, connect it to the skill of give and take.

Choosing to Be Responsible

LEARNING OBJECTIVES

Students will:

- realize they are responsible for their own actions
- see the connection between responsibility and cooperation

MATERIALS NEEDED

The book *It's Not Fair!* by Carl Sommer, "Bee Responsible Bookmark" activity sheet (page 164), markers, construction paper, pencils, scissors, and glue

LESSON PLAN

READ   *It's Not Fair*. Buzzie Bee overhears some disturbing news. She becomes furious and starts a revolt among the younger bees. The story emphasizes the values of citizenship, teamwork, and responsibility.

An optional text for teacher shared reading is *Sheila Rae, the Brave* by Kevin Henkes. Sheila decides to go home from school a different way. When Sheila gets lost and her courage falters, her little sister Louise proves her bravery by leading her sister safely home.

DISCUSS   What happens when people get angry and don't think about the consequences of their actions? In the story, who was responsible for the bees leaving the hive? Why did Buzzie want to leave? What choice did the bees make to solve the problem? Define *responsibility* and *dependability*. Discuss what it means to be responsible for your own actions. Review different ways students can be responsible. Discuss the importance of people being able to count on one another.

DO   the "Bee Responsible Bookmark" activity. Use the templates on the activity sheet to make bee bookmarks, which can serve as frequent reminders for the kids to be responsible. Help the students add a personal message to the bookmark, such as "I am responsible" or "I can *bee* responsible." After constructing the bookmarks, arrange to laminate them for more durability.

RELATE   responsibility to cooperative behavior. When students cooperate with others (kids and adults) and with the rules of the school, they are acting responsibly. Let the students know how much you appreciate it when they choose to be helpful and responsible. Use their bookmarks as constant reminders to be responsible by making good choices that support cooperation.

Safe & Caring Sun

LEARNING OBJECTIVES

Students will:

- learn to make choices that help them get along with others
- recognize that "fair" does not always mean the same thing to everyone

MATERIALS NEEDED

The book *Jamaica's Blue Marker* by Juanita Havill, "Safe & Caring Sun" activity sheet (page 165), pencils or pens, and crayons or markers

LESSON PLAN

READ *Jamaica's Blue Marker*. Jamaica is not thrilled about having to share her blue marker with Russell, especially when he takes the marker and draws all over her picture. Jamaica makes the right choice when she learns why Russell behaves the way he does.

> An optional text for teacher shared reading is *It's Not Fair!* by Anita Harper. For the big sister, putting up with a baby brother is not fair until she begins to understand the ups and downs of having a new sibling.

DISCUSS Review the story and discuss how the characters felt. Brainstorm with the kids their ideas for getting along with others. What is fair? Why did Jamaica change her mind and feelings about Russell?

DO the "Safe & Caring Sun" activity sheet. Children use the word list to complete the sentences and write them on the sun (*I listen to others. I wait for my turn. I like to share. I say please and thank you. I help my friends. I use my kind words. I care about others.*) Color and cut out the suns to make a bright wall display.

RELATE Children usually want everything to be "fair." In their eyes, fair may mean equal treatment of everyone. Sometimes what is fair for one person, is not fair for another. Provide examples from your classroom or school. In order to be fair, sometimes we have to look at the different expectations and the different circumstances surrounding a situation before judging if something is fair.

Growing Responsibility

LEARNING OBJECTIVES

Students will:

- review what it means to be responsible
- brainstorm ideas of how to be responsible citizens within the classroom

MATERIALS NEEDED

The book *Jason Takes Responsibility* by Virginia Kroll, "Growing Responsibility" activity sheet (page 166), green construction paper, scissors, markers, green yarn, and tape

LESSON PLAN

READ *Jason Takes Responsibility*. Jason loves to help others, but one day when his mom asks him to do something important, something goes wrong and Jason has to make a decision about what to do.

> An optional text for teacher shared reading is *The Tale of Custard the Dragon* by Ogden Nash. Custard cowers in fear until a nasty pirate shows up and brings out his dragon instincts.

DISCUSS What is *responsibility?* What kind of things did Jason do to help? What happened when Jason went to mail the invitations? Why didn't he tell the truth to his mom right away? What did he choose to do at the end of the story?

DO the "Growing Responsibility" activity. Start by creating a class list of ways children can be responsible in the classroom and at school. Then have the kids choose items from the list that reflect how they have been responsible this year. Write these on the plant leaves on their activity sheets. Talk about how the children have grown in their ability to be responsible during the year. Have each student copy one item from her or his activity sheet onto a green leaf cut from construction paper. On a bulletin board, make a vine from green yarn to which the kids can glue their leaves. Title the board "Growing Responsibility" and add leaves as the kids show their responsibility skills.

RELATE this activity to the fact that as we grow, we are given more responsibility because we learn how to be more caring and are able to make good choices. From now until the end of the school year, each time a child makes a good choice and is responsible, he or she can add a leaf to the vine. Watch it grow!

The Power to Choose Quiz

Use the quiz activity sheet (page 167) to review and assess what the students learned this month. *(Answers: 1-T, 2-T, 3-T, 4-F, 5-T, 6-others, 7-think, 8-problems, work, 9-responsible)*

"The infraction rate at school has dropped significantly. The infraction rate is the day-to-day business of what's going on in school. I can see that there's a change of the day-to-day business of children being nasty to each other and children not listening to the teacher. All of the small infractions added up is a big problem, and decreasing them has made a big difference."

PRINCIPAL—TARBOX SCHOOL

SAFE & CARING
VOCABULARY BUILDER

Word Find

K	U	R	P	O	W	E	R
N	L	F	Y	P	R	S	K
H	O	A	A	H	T	O	G
E	V	I	T	I	S	O	P
O	C	U	S	V	R	H	I
L	R	N	S	I	R	C	D
T	H	I	N	K	C	R	A
A	R	C	I	B	L	E	K
Z	G	E	N	T	L	E	D

Circle these words in the Word Find puzzle.
(Hint: Words can run up, down, forward, backward, or diagonally.)

Key Words:

FAIR

TALK

NICE

THINK

TRUTH

Challenge Words:

CHOOSE

DECISION

GENTLE

POSITIVE

POWER

Use the words from above to fill in the blanks and complete the sentences.

We have the _____ to make choices.

We are responsible for speaking the _____ .

When we _____ about our feelings, it helps us get along.

A _____ decision is a _____ choice to make.

we are
a safe
& caring
SCHOOL.

MY CHOICES

APRIL

	😃 Good Choices	🙁 Poor Choices
Monday		
Tuesday		
Wednesday		
Thursday		
Friday		
Saturday		
Sunday		

we are
a safe
& caring
school.

POSITIVE CHOICE!

Draw a picture story about a time you made a great choice!

we are a safe & caring school.

WHAT COULD HAPPEN?

The Situation: It's time for lunch at school and your class is moving very slowly to the cafeteria.

Your choices are:
 1) Run ahead of your class to get in line sooner.
 2) Stay with your class and take your turn.

The consequences of those choices are:

To make the best choice, think about what the consequences might be.

The choice I would make is _____

_____

_____

we aRe
a safe
& CaRiNG
SCHOOL.

TELLING OR TATTLING?

Suki got cut on the playground and is bleeding.

You run to find an adult.

○ **Telling?**
or
○ **Tattling?**

Why?

_____
_____
_____

Marcus sees the principal speaking to another student from his class.

He runs to find his teacher.

○ **Telling?**
or
○ **Tattling?**

Why?

_____
_____
_____

Chris sees Amela take one bite from her apple and throw it away.

He runs to find an adult.

○ **Telling?**
or
○ **Tattling?**

Why?

_____
_____
_____

Jorge sees Melissa kick Jonathon in the shins.

He runs to find an adult.

○ **Telling?**
or
○ **Tattling?**

Why?

_____
_____
_____

Maria and Alexis are screaming at each other in the restroom.

You run to find an adult.

○ **Telling?**
or
○ **Tattling?**

Why?

_____
_____
_____

we aRe a saFe & CaRiNG SCHOOL.

From *Activities for Building Character and Social-Emotional Learning Grades 1–2* by Katia S. Petersen, Ph.D., copyright © 2012. Free Spirit Publishing Inc., Minneapolis, MN; 800-735-7323; www.freespirit.com.
This page may be reproduced for individual, classroom, and small group work only. For all other uses, contact www.freespirit.com/company/permissions.cfm.

 **AUTHOR FOR A DAY**

_____

Title

By _____

_____

_____

_____

_____

_____

_____

_____

_____

_____

_____

_____

_____

_____

_____

We ARE
a SAFE
& CARiNG
SCHOOL.

Give and Take

Write in the speech bubbles how students might work things out

1 Maria and Helen always get to the swings first. You really want to have a turn. How can you work it out?

2 There are three pieces of pizza left, but there are two of you. How can you work it out?

3 You both need to use the same computer. How can you work it out?

4 You want to play a game, but your friend wants to watch a movie. How can you work it out?

We are a safe & caring school.

BEE RESPONSIBLE BOOKMARK

Using this pattern, trace and draw on colored paper to make a bee with a yellow and black body, black head, and white wings. Glue the bee parts to the paper strip to complete your Bee Bookmark.

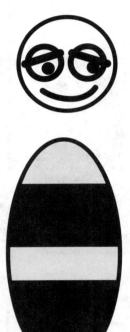

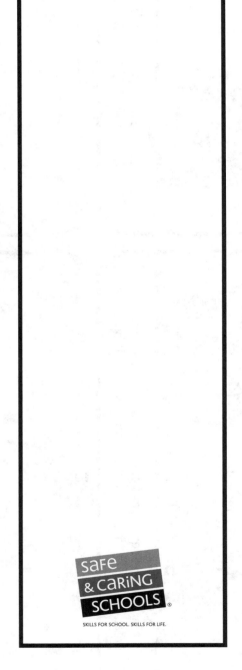

SAFE & CARING SCHOOLS

SKILLS FOR SCHOOL. SKILLS FOR LIFE.

WE ARE a SAFE & CARING SCHOOL.

safe & caring sun

Use words from the list to fill in the blanks in the sentences.

wait	care	I _____ to others.
help	kind	I _____ for my _____.
share	use	I like to _____.
words	turn	I say _____ and _____ ____.
listen	thank you	I _____ my friends.
please		I ____ my _____ _____.
		I _____ about others.

Copy the sentences onto the rays of the sun.

GROWING RESPONSIBILITY

APRIL

Name

we are
a safe
& caring
SCHOOL.

THE POWER TO CHOOSE QUIZ

True or False (circle the correct answer)

1) I have the power to choose. .... **True / False**

2) Making good choices is sometimes hard. .... **True / False**

3) When I don't know what to do, I can get help. .... **True / False**

4) Just make any choice; thinking about choices
doesn't help. .... **True / False**

5) I can choose to do the right thing. .... **True / False**

Fill in the Blanks

Unscramble the words to complete the sentences.

6) We should try to be fair with _____.
h s o e t r

7) Stopping to _____ helps us make good choices.
i h n k t

8) Even friends have _____, but we can _____ them out.
e o s l r m b p   w r k o

9) Being _____ is a good choice to make.
e p n i l r s o s b e

Draw or write

10) Tell about a time you made a positive choice.

we are a safe & caring SCHOOL.

"Safe & Caring Schools is very much a part of everything I do. In my classroom, we constantly talk about the choices that we make, out interactions with other people, and what results from making good choices versus making bad choices we would regret. We talk a lot about personal responsibility, and all of that is so much a part of Safe & Caring Schools."

TEACHER—SOUTH LAWRENCE EAST SCHOOL

SKILLS FOR SCHOOL. SKILLS FOR LIFE.

MAY
Follow Your Dreams

- **Goal Setting**
- **Perseverance**

- **Celebration of Self and Others**

In order for children to reach for their dreams, they need to recognize their strengths and abilities. They deserve our ongoing support and constant reminders that we believe in them. They need to see the relevance of school and how social and emotional learning is a key part of their development.

MONTHLY OBJECTIVES
Students will:

- understand the importance of persistence and a positive attitude in facing challenges in school and life
- realize that having dreams and hopes helps them plan for the future
- learn how to set goals and plan the steps to achieve them
- evaluate and celebrate their growth and success during the school year

TEACHING TIPS

- Help children connect new learning to real-life experiences.
- Encourage the power of young minds by stirring their imagination through creative play, thinking, and writing.
- Improve children's well-being by letting them know you believe in them.
- Success brings more success. Recognize small accomplishments on a daily basis.

MAY INTEGRATED ACTIVITIES

In addition to the specific lesson plans for this month, you can use these optional ideas to integrate and extend the Safe & Caring themes into daily routines and across the curricular areas.

LANGUAGE ARTS

- Have students write short stories about their dreams for the future (when they grow up). Collect the stories. Read a few each day. Ask students to guess whose dreams they learned about. This activity reinforces the fact that everyone can have hopes and dreams.
- Read *Brave Irene* by William Steig. When reviewing the story with your students, ask them to help Irene find solutions to each challenge she faces.

LITERATURE

- Visit the library to look for books that explore an individual's gifts and talents. Have students draw pictures, create collages, or write short stories about their own gifts and talents. Some books to consider are: *Clarissa* by Carol Talley, *I'm Terrific* by Marjorie Weinman Sharmat, *A Color of His Own* by Leo Lionni.
- Read *The Three Questions* by Jon J. Muth, a story about growing up and learning how to do the right thing. Kids can share their own ideas and stories about what they would like to learn as they get older.

SOCIAL STUDIES

- Invite parents and community guests to share information about their jobs.
- Organize a career day, and help students dress up like people in different jobs. Discuss how these jobs are important in the community.
- Read *Community Helpers from A to Z* by Bobbie Kalman. Photos of people in real-life jobs represent the important contribution each makes to the community.

ART

- Read *My Name Is Georgia: A Portrait* by Jeanette Winter. Students can explore their own dreams using beautiful, bright colors, just like Georgia O'Keefe has done in her paintings.
- Read *Picasso and the Girl with a Ponytail* by Laurence Anholt. A shy girl learns to believe in herself, and she becomes a famous painter.
- Create a classroom book called "Following Your Dreams." Have students write and draw pictures about their dreams and ways they can reach them.
- Read *The Little Engine That Could* by Watty Piper. Students work as a team to decorate a shoebox to look like the little engine. Later, when they have a problem or need help doing something, the students can write a private note to the teacher and drop it in the box.
- Have students draw pictures of what they would like to be when they grow up.

MUSIC

- Listen to the song "I'm Not Perfect" from *The Best of the Laurie Berkner Band* (www .laurieberkner .com) or songs from the CD *Free to Be . . . You and Me* by Marlo Thomas and Friends (www.freetobefoundation.org). Discuss song lyrics about trying hard and self-esteem.

MATH

- Read *Just Enough Carrots* by Stuart J. Murphy. Elephants, rabbits, and birds shop in an unusual grocery store. Reinforce the fact that learning math skills can contribute to achieving goals and dreams for the future.

Safe & Caring Schools Vocabulary Builder

LEARNING OBJECTIVES

Students will:

- be introduced to vocabulary that supports making and achieving goals
- internalize the vocabulary as they use it throughout the month and year in real-life situations

MATERIALS NEEDED

"Safe & Caring Vocabulary Builder" activity sheet (page 176) and pencils

LESSON PLAN

Use the vocabulary activities to introduce the concepts and common language associated with this month's theme. Throughout the month, use the words in writing, spelling, storytelling, and dealing with conflict situations. Add the words to your word wall.

For the Word Find activity, choose to use the key words, challenge words, or both. Complete the activity and discuss what the words mean to the students. You may want students to work in pairs to help each other.

For the fill-in-the-blanks activity, students complete the words by filling in the missing vowels (*gifts, job, fun, skills, talent, career, steps, hope, dreams*).

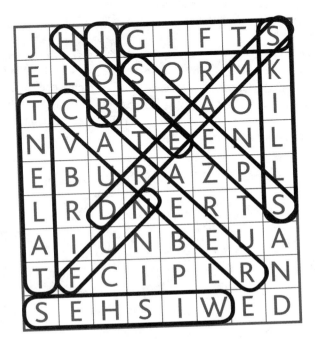

My Gifts and Talents

LEARNING OBJECTIVES

Students will:

- recognize their individual gifts and talents
- explore different ways to use their talents

MATERIALS NEEDED

The book *Willa the Wonderful* by Susan Milord, "My Gifts and Talents" activity sheet (page 177), pencils or pens, and crayons or markers

LESSON PLAN

READ Willa the Wonderful. When Willa announces her career goal to be a fairy princess, her family and friends are skeptical. One day something big happens, and Willa discovers she can be a fairy princess in her own unique way.

> An optional text for teacher shared reading is *Lentil* by Robert McCloskey. Lentil's harmonica playing saves the day when calamity threatens the homecoming celebration for the leading citizen of Alto, Ohio.

DISCUSS Explain to the children that we all have different gifts and talents. Some of us are great at singing or dancing; others are good at drawing or sports; others are good readers. Help children realize that their gifts and talents are important and make them special.

DO the "My Gifts and Talents" activity sheet. Children start by identifying their favorite things. They may be very good at these things, or their skills may still be developing. Complete the sheet with the writing and drawing activity. Once the children complete the activity sheet, ask them to complete the following sentence: If my talent is _____, I could grow up to be _____.

RELATE Reinforce the point that everyone has unique talents and abilities. While the students have many talents, not everyone wants to do the same things. Share and compare the students' activity sheets. Explain that all gifts and talents are valued and celebrated in a safe and caring classroom.

What's My Job?

LEARNING OBJECTIVES

Students will:

- become aware of different career opportunities in their community
- learn about some of the choices they will have as they grow up

MATERIALS NEEDED

The book *Matthew's Dream* by Leo Lionni and "What's My Job?" activity sheet (page 178)

LESSON PLAN

READ *Matthew's Dream.* A visit to an art museum inspires a young mouse to become an artist, despite the wishes of his parents who want him to become a doctor.

An optional text for teacher shared reading is *Dooby Dooby Moo* by Doreen Cronin. When Duck discovers an ad in the paper announcing a talent show at the county fair, Farmer Brown's animals are unstoppable.

DISCUSS When Matthew's parents asked him what he wants to be when he grows up, what did he say? What was Matthew's dream? What did Matthew decide to become when he grows up? Brainstorm jobs people do around the school, in neighborhoods, or at home. Discuss what a baker does, a bus driver, a doctor, a teacher, and other professions.

DO the "What's My Job?" activity by playing 10 Questions with the careers from the activity sheet. Choose a job card and give the children one clue, such as "I wear a special hat." The children can ask questions that can only be answered with a "yes" or "no" to help them figure out the job. For an optional activity, play charades with the careers or have the children give clues to help others guess the job.

RELATE this lesson to real life by pointing out that the students can grow up to do just about anything they want. What they like now may change by the time they graduate from high school and start a job or a career path. The important thing is to have dreams and to try to be the best they can be.

When I Grow Up, I Want to Be. . .

LEARNING OBJECTIVES

Students will:

- consider different careers that might be right for them
- learn how they might follow their dreams

MATERIALS NEEDED

The book *When I Grow Up* by P. K. Hallinan, "When I Grow Up, I Want to Be..." activity sheet (page 179), pencils or pens, and crayons or markers

LESSON PLAN

READ *When I Grow Up.* A child ponders possible occupations from A (actor) to Z (zookeeper).

An optional text for teacher shared reading is *Career Day* by Anne Rockwell. Each of 10 children in this book introduces a parent or grandparent who talks about his or her occupation.

DISCUSS the many things the students might want to be as they grow up. Talk about how important it is to have dreams, but to be open to the fact that those dreams will likely change as the children grow older. No one has to be locked into one choice at this age.

DO the "When I Grow Up, I Want to Be..." activity sheet. Students are to draw a picture of what they would like to be when they grow up and write a sentence or paragraph about it.

RELATE Review the book you read and the many job opportunities from which students can choose. What new jobs do the kids think will be created in the next five to ten years? Share their pictures and sentences from the activity sheet. Let the kids know that they never need to be afraid to try something new.

Working on a Dream

LEARNING OBJECTIVES

Students will:

- set a goal and take the necessary steps to reach it
- learn about perseverance and determination

MATERIALS NEEDED

The book *Brave Irene* by William Steig, "Working on a Dream" activity sheet (page 180), and pencils or pens

LESSON PLAN

READ   *Brave Irene.* Irene, a dressmaker's daughter, braves a snowstorm to deliver a gown to the duchess.

An optional text for teacher shared reading is *Little Toot* by Hardie Gramatky. Little Toot, the tugboat, conquers his fear of rough seas when he single-handedly rescues an ocean liner during a storm.

DISCUSS   Why did Irene have to go out into the storm? How did she feel when walking through the storm? How did Irene feel when she finally delivered the gown? Explain to the children that we all have things to improve upon, things like getting better at cleaning our room, being a better listener, following directions, keeping our hands to ourselves, or being a better friend. Remind students that in order to get better at something, we have to make a plan and practice. We can't give up when things get tough.

DO   the "Working on a Dream" activity sheet. Ask children if they have a goal they would like to work on. Have students brainstorm ideas of what they would like to improve or attain. Help them create goals and think about the steps they need to take to reach those goals. Have them write the goals in the "dream or goal" section of the sheet. Then have them think about and write the steps they need to take to accomplish that goal. If your students are not accustomed to writing goals, demonstrate this process by doing the activity on an overhead transparency. Set a class goal and record the steps the class can take to attain the goal.

RELATE   the goal-setting activity to other things the students do that may seem very difficult at first. Let the children know that no matter how hard something may be, they should never give up. Reiterate the importance of practicing and continually trying until they succeed. Remind them that you and others will be there to help them.

Climbing High!

LEARNING OBJECTIVES

Students will:

- understand that it takes motivation and determination to accomplish anything
- learn that persevering means to stick with a task until it is completed

MATERIALS NEEDED

The book *The Little Red Ant and the Great Big Crumb* by Shirley Climo, "Climbing High!" activity sheet (page 181), and pencils or pens

LESSON PLAN

READ   *The Little Red Ant and the Great Big Crumb.* A tiny ant finds a crumb that is too heavy to lift and searches for help. After seeking different animals, she discovers who is really the strongest.

An optional text for teacher shared reading is *Froggy Learns to Swim* by Jonathan London. Froggy is afraid of the water until his mother, with flippers, snorkle, and mask, helps him learn to swim.

DISCUSS   Help the children make a connection between the story and times when they felt like giving up. Remind them that it's okay to ask for help. Have the class practice saying out loud, "I will do my best." Recognize students for their efforts.

DO   the "Climbing High!" activity sheet. Before copying the sheet, be sure to add the assignments the children are to complete in the racks. (If individualizing the assignments, print the sheet first.) Explain that each time the students complete an assignment, they color the rock on the hill, keeping in mind the goal is to complete all four assignments.

RELATE   the lesson of not giving up to the students' lives at school. Explain how learning is sometimes a difficult task that may take several tries to complete. Remind them that you will help them when they feel like giving up.

I Am a Star

LEARNING OBJECTIVES

Students will:

- practice making good choices
- learn that positive outcomes will likely result when they make good choices

MATERIALS NEEDED

The book *Stand Tall, Molly Lou Melon* by Patty Lovell, "I Am a Star" activity sheet (page 182), digital camera, and star stickers

LESSON PLAN

READ   *Stand Tall, Molly Lou Melon*. Even when the class bully at her new school makes fun of her, Molly remembers what her grandmother told her and feels good about herself.

> An optional text for teacher shared reading is *Fritz and the Beautiful Horses* by Jan Brett. Fritz, a pony excluded from the group of beautiful horses becomes a hero when he rescues the children of the city.

DISCUSS   How did the bully treat Molly Lou Melon? How did Molly Lou feel about it? What helped her remember how special she is? Explain to the children that every day they have another chance to make good choices. Making good choices helps everyone get along better.

DO   the "I Am a Star" activity sheet. Use a digital camera to take photos of the students to place in the center of the stars. Tell students that each time they make a good choice, you will give them star stickers to place on their sheets. At the end of each week, students count their stars. Add up the class total to see how many good choices they made that week.

RELATE   the number of good choices the class made to the students' abilities to choose wisely in school and in life. For making good choices, each student is a star and deserves recognition. Send the star sheets home with the children, and include a note telling the parents how their children are shining stars for making good choices.

Looking Up to My Hero

LEARNING OBJECTIVES

Students will:

- identify people they look up to as heroes
- learn the qualities that make someone great

MATERIALS NEEDED

The book *If Only I Could!* by David and Mutiya Vision, "Looking Up to My Hero" activity sheet (page 183), pencils or pens, and crayons or markers

LESSON PLAN

READ   *If Only I Could!* The child in the story gets upset and wants to quit when things don't go as planned. She discovers that even though learning new things calls for perseverance, it can also be fun.

> An optional text for teacher shared reading is *The Tortoise and the Hare: An Aesop's Fable* retold by Angela McAllister. This tale pits boastfulness and conceit against sharp wits and doggedness.

DISCUSS   the meaning of heroes. What do heroes say or do that we like? What do we learn from them? Who are some of the people we care about that make us proud? Conclude with a definition for *heroes (people we look up to because of what they stand for or have accomplished, making us feel proud)*.

DO   the "Looking Up to My Hero" activity sheet. Students draw a picture of one person they look up to, write what that person does that makes her or him great, and write the qualities the student would like to emulate.

RELATE   the lesson to what the children have learned this year. Is there anyone within the school that the class considers a hero? Maybe it is the custodian who always cleans up after them in the lunchroom, or the physical education teacher who is always encouraging them, or the aide who volunteers her time to help, or the music teacher who teaches them to sing. Everyday heroes are everywhere.

My Book About Practice

LEARNING OBJECTIVES

Students will:

- discover the powerful results of practice
- determine what they need to practice

MATERIALS NEEDED

The book *Ronald Morgan Goes to Bat* by Patricia Reilly Giff, "My Book About Practice" activity sheet (page 184), pencils or pens, and crayons or markers

LESSON PLAN

READ *Ronald Morgan Goes to Bat*. Ronald has great team spirit, and he tries hard to be a good player. Initially, he is discouraged because he has trouble hitting the ball, Ronald eventually figures out what he needs to do.

> An optional text for teacher shared reading is *The Most Wonderful Egg in the World* by Helme Heine. Three hens go to the king to see who is the most beautiful. The king challenges them to a contest to see who will be made a princess.

DISCUSS How did Ronald feel when he could not hit the ball? What did he try to do to help his team? How did his friends feel? Ask children what kinds of things they need to practice. Why it is important to practice?

DO the "My Book About Practice" activity sheet. The students will write a story about something they need to practice so they can improve their skill. For the cover of the book, have them draw a picture of themselves practicing. Cut out the finished pages and staple them into a book.

RELATE the importance of practicing to the many things in life students will have to do or try. Remind them that few people are really good at a new thing the first time they try it. If you want to be good, you have to practice. Name some people who probably practice a lot to be successful at what they do *(a piano player, a golfer, a doctor, a truck driver)*.

My Great Year!

LEARNING OBJECTIVES

Students will:

- learn to recognize their accomplishments
- celebrate their school year

MATERIALS NEEDED

The book *Emily's Art* by Peter Catalanotto, "My Great Year!" activity sheet (page 185), pencils or pens, and crayons or markers

LESSON PLAN

READ *Emily's Art*. When Emily's first-grade teacher announces an art contest for which a judge will choose the best entry, Emily is skeptical.

> An optional text for teacher shared reading is *Molly the Brave and Me* by Jane O'Connor. Beth admires her friend Molly's courage. On a visit to Molly's country home, Beth surprises herself with her own bravery when the two become lost in a cornfield.

DISCUSS Why was Emily skeptical about the art contest? What did she do? Celebrating success is a wonderful thing to do no matter how big or small the success. Help children review significant milestones they accomplished this year, either as a group or individually.

DO the "My Great Year!" activity sheet. Students fill in the top half with answers to the prompts. On the bottom half, they draw or write four things they did that made them feel proud of themselves.

RELATE Identify the many things that have made you proud to be the students' teacher this year. Compare that to what the students wrote on the activity sheets. Let the students know you have seen them grow in many ways. Celebrate the accomplishments of the children and encourage them to continue to work hard, practice, set goals for themselves, make good choices, and succeed in school.

Follow Your Dreams Quiz

Use the quiz activity sheet (page 186) to review and assess what the students learned this month. *(Answers: 1-T, 2-F, 3-T, 4-F, 5-T, 6-goal, 7-star, 8-dream, 9-anything)*

Safe & Caring
Vocabulary Builder

Word Find Puzzle

J	H	J	G	I	F	T	S	S
E	L	O	S	O	R	M	K	
T	C	B	P	T	A	O	I	
N	V	A	T	E	E	N	L	
E	B	U	R	A	Z	P	L	
L	R	D	N	E	R	T	S	
A	I	U	N	B	E	U	A	
T	F	C	I	P	L	R	N	
S	E	H	S	I	W	E	D	

Circle these words in the Word Find puzzle.
(Hint: Words can run up, down, forward, backward, or diagonally.)

Key Words:
FUN
HOPE
GIFTS
JOB
SKILLS

Challenge Words:
CAREER
DREAMS
STEPS
TALENT
WISHES

Fill in the blanks with vowels to complete the words.

g _ fts   sk _ lls   st _ ps

j _ b   t _ l _ nt   h _ pe

f _ n   c _ r _ _ r   dr _ _ ms

we are
a safe
& caring
school.

MAY

My Gifts and Talents

Circle your favorite things to do!

 bike

 read

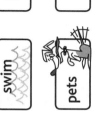 swim

 pets

 sing

 sports

 draw

 skate

Write a story and draw a picture of your favorite things to do.

I can do lots of great stuff!

we are a safe a caring & SCHOOL

WHAT'S MY JOB?

Airplane Pilot	Teacher	Athlete
Firefighter	Photographer	Doctor
Construction Worker	Painter	Cowboy
Ambulance Driver	Musician	Nurse
Astronaut	Police Officer	Baker

we are a safe & caring school.

WHEN I GROW UP, I WANT TO BE...

Draw

Write

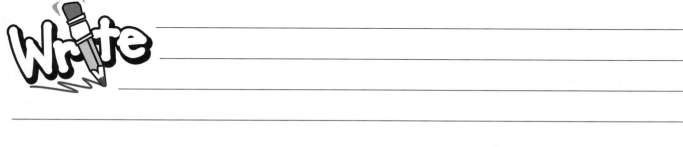

we are
a safe
& caring
school.

Working on a Dream

Step 1

Step 2

Step 3

Dream or Goal

CLIMBING HIGH!

Your goal is to climb to the top.

Color each rock when you complete the task, and sign your name once you reach the peak.

Start here

MAY

Your name

Assignment 1

Assignment 2

Assignment 3

Assignment 4

From *Activities for Building Character and Social-Emotional Learning Grades 1–2* by Katia S. Petersen, Ph.D., copyright © 2012. Free Spirit Publishing Inc., Minneapolis, MN; 800-735-7323; www.freespirit.com.
This page may be reproduced for individual, classroom, and small group work only. For all other uses, contact www.freespirit.com/company/permissions.cfm.

I AM A STAR

Student's
Photo

WE ARE
A SAFE
& CARING
SCHOOL.

LOOKING UP TO MY HERO

Our heroes can be anyone we admire.

Our heroes show us great things we can do.

Who is someone you look up to?

Name

What makes your hero great?

What can you do to be more like your hero?

Draw a picture of your hero.

We are a safe & caring school.

At the end...

_____
_____
_____
_____
_____
_____
_____
_____
_____

MY BOOK ABOUT PRACTICE

by _____

_____
_____
_____
_____
_____
_____
_____
_____
_____
_____

...and then...

_____
_____
_____
_____
_____
_____
_____
_____
_____

One day...

we are a safe & caring school.

MY GREAT YEAR!

My favorite books
I read:

_____
_____
_____
_____
_____
_____

Something new
I learned:

_____
_____
_____
_____
_____
_____

Some of the fun
things we did:

_____
_____
_____
_____
_____
_____

One thing I did to make my school a safe and caring place:

_____

Draw or write two things you did this year that made you feel proud.

we are
a safe
& caring
school.

FOLLOW YOUR DREAMS QUIZ

True or False (circle the correct answer)

1) Heroes help me think about my goals. .... **True / False**

2) Practice is only for wimps. .... **True / False**

3) We can work in teams to reach our dreams. .... **True / False**

4) I don't need goals. .... **True / False**

5) I should practice the skills I need to succeed. .... **True / False**

Fill in the Blanks

Use these letters: a, d, e, g, h, i, n, o, t, y to complete the words.

6) Don't give up on an important __ __al.

7) I am a s__ __r for trying new things.

8) I can go far with a __r__am and good choices.

9) I can be an__t__ __ __g I want to be.

Draw or Write

10) Tell about a dream you want to achieve.

From *Activities for Building Character and Social-Emotional Learning Grades 1–2* by Katia S. Petersen, Ph.D., copyright © 2012. Free Spirit Publishing Inc., Minneapolis, MN; 800-735-7323; www.freespirit.com.
This page may be reproduced for individual, classroom, and small group work only. For all other uses, contact www.freespirit.com/company/permissions.cfm.

"One way that I'm able to integrate Safe & Caring Schools is through read-alouds. We connect the story we read to the children's lives by asking how the character in the book addressed the issue and how the children would address the issue. It's really become the central part of my classroom, and as a result the children have developed better bonds with each other."

TEACHER—SOUTH LAWRENCE EAST SCHOOL

RECOMMENDED RESOURCES

BOOKS

All Kids Are Our Kids: What Communities Must Do to Raise Caring and Responsible Children and Adolescents by Peter L. Benson (San Francisco: Jossey-Bass, 1997). Challenges all community members to take responsibility for the development and well-being of the community's children. Emphasizes asset building.

Building Academic Success on Social and Emotional Learning: What Does the Research Say? edited by Joseph E. Zins, Roger P. Weissberg, Margaret C. Wang, and Herbert J. Walberg (New York: Teachers College Press, 2004). Explains the science and research supporting the integration of social and emotional learning (SEL) into school curriculum.

Caring Classrooms/Intelligent Schools: The Social Emotional Education of Young Children edited by Jonathan Cohen (New York: Teachers College Press, 2001). Experts provide tips and strategies for integrating SEL into the school day.

Educating Minds and Hearts: Social Emotional Learning and the Passage into Adolescence edited by Jonathan Cohen (New York: Teachers College Press, 1999). Explains the theory and science supporting SEL and provides overviews of successful SEL programs across the nation.

Emotional Intelligence: Why It Can Matter More than I.Q. by Daniel P. Goleman (New York: Bantam Books, 2006). Explains how and why emotional intelligence is a key factor in determining career success, relationship satisfaction, overall well-being, and more.

Emotionally Intelligent Parenting: How to Raise a Self-Disciplined, Responsible, Socially Skilled Child by Maurice J. Elias, Steve E. Tobias, and Brian S. Friedlander (New York: Harmony Books, 1997). Contains advice and practical strategies on how to foster emotional intelligence in children.

Higher Expectations: Promoting Social Emotional Learning and Academic Achievement in Your School by Raymond J. Pasi (New York: Teachers College Press, 2001). Helpful advice on how to design and implement a successful SEL program in your classroom, school, and school district.

Multiple Intelligences: The Theory in Practice by Howard Gardner (New York: Basic Books, 1993). Practical applications of multiple intelligence theory for educators.

The New Bully Free Classroom by Allan L. Beane (Minneapolis: Free Spirit Publishing, 2011). More than 100 bullying prevention and intervention strategies for teachers of grades K–8.

Promoting Social and Emotional Learning: Guidelines for Educators by Maurice J. Elias (Alexandria, VA: Association for Supervision and Curriculum Development, 1997). Advice on how to advocate for, develop, implement, and evaluate school-wide SEL programs.

Raising a Thinking Child: Help Your Child to Resolve Everyday Conflicts and Get Along with Others by Myrna B. Shure with Theresa Foy DiGeronimo (New York: Henry Holt, 1994). Tips for helping kids become independent thinkers with the self-esteem, self-confidence, and problem-solving skills to handle challenges throughout life.

Raising a Thinking Preteen: The "I Can Problem Solve" Program for 8- to 12-Year-Olds by Myrna B. Shure with Roberta Israeloff (New York: Henry Holt: 2000). Advice for fostering independent thinking, problem-solving skills, and self-confidence in tweens.

Resiliency: What We Have Learned by Bonnie Benard (San Francisco: WestEd, 2004). Summarizes ten years of research on resiliency development in children and offers suggestions on how to incorporate and apply the research in everyday life.

Service Learning in the PreK–3 Classroom: The What, Why, and How-To Guide for Every Teacher by Vickie E. Lake and Ithel Jones (Minneapolis: Free Spirit Publishing, 2012). A comprehensive, research-based guide helps early childhood professionals implement service learning across the primary grade curriculum.

What Kids Need to Succeed: Proven, Practical Ways to Raise Good Kids (**Revised and Updated 3rd Edition**) by Peter L. Benson, Judy Galbraith, and Pamela Espeland (Minneapolis: Free Spirit Publishing, 2012). Over 900 suggestions to help adults build Developmental Assets in children at home, at school, and in the community.

ORGANIZATIONS/WEBSITES

Character Education Partnership (CEP)
1025 Connecticut Avenue NW, Suite 1011
Washington, DC 20036
800-988-8081
www.character.org
A nonprofit organization dedicated to promoting character education at all grade levels. The website contains downloadable publications, lesson plans, a character education blog, and a substantive list of resources.

Collaborative for Academic, Social, and Emotional Learning (CASEL)
University of Illinois at Chicago
Department of Psychology
815 West Van Buren Street, Suite 210
Chicago, IL 60607
312-226-3770
www.casel.org
An organization dedicated to promoting and advancing the practice of SEL. The website offers information and resources on all aspects of SEL advocacy and implementation.

Educators for Social Responsibility (ESR)
23 Garden Street
Cambridge, MA 02138
800-370-2515
www.esrnational.org
A national nonprofit organization that works with educators to advocate practices such as SEL, character development, conflict resolution, diversity education, civic engagement, and more. The website contains lesson plans, activities, articles, and links for teachers of all grades.

GoodCharacter.com
www.goodcharacter.com
Recommended by the Parents' Choice Foundation, this website contains resources for character development and service learning. Includes articles, tips, teaching guides, lesson plans, and resource lists.

Learning Peace
www.learningpeace.com
This site helps educators, parents, and other adults create more peace in schools, homes, and communities by teaching children conflict resolution, anger management, anti-bullying, and character building.

National School Climate Center (NSCC)
548 8th Avenue, Rm 930
New York, NY 10018
212-707-8799
www.schoolclimate.org
The NSCC is an organization that helps schools integrate crucial social and emotional learning with academic instruction.

Search Institute
The Banks Building
615 First Avenue NE, Suite 125
Minneapolis, MN 55413
800-888-7828
www.search-institute.org
Through dynamic research and analysis, this independent nonprofit organization works to promote healthy, active, and content youth and communities through asset building.

Teaching Tolerance
The Southern Poverty Law Center
400 Washington Avenue
Montgomery, AL 36104
334-956-8200
www.tolerance.org
A national education project dedicated to helping teachers foster respect and understanding in the classroom. The website contains resources for educators, parents, teens, and kids.

WestEd
730 Harrison Street
San Francisco, CA 94107
877-493-7833
www.wested.org
A nonprofit research, development, and service agency, WestEd enhances and increases education and human development within schools, families, and communities.

ABOUT THE AUTHOR

Katia S. Petersen, Ph.D., is an author, consultant, and educator. She is a training expert in school climate improvement, student support, teacher coaching, and parent engagement. She has delivered professional development courses in schools nationwide on how to use literature to infuse social and emotional learning into core academics. Katia has trained over 65,000 educators and parents to enhance school success.

Katia has received many accolades and awards for her work with children and schools. They include having her books named in the "Top Ten Books" by the National Association of Elementary School Principals; being honored with a Teacher's Choice: Excellence in the Classroom Award from *Teacher Magazine*; and winning the National Association of Broadcasters Service to Children's Television Award.

Katia is the creator of the Safe & Caring Schools program for grades preK–8. She is the president and founder of Petersen Argo, Inc., a consulting firm that has been serving the educational needs of children and adults since 1990. She lives with her family in San Francisco, California.

For more information about Katia, the Safe & Caring Schools program, and training opportunities, check out www.safeandcaringschools.com.

INDEX

Note: Activity names are in **bold**; reproducible sheets have a **bold** page number.

NOTES

NOTES

Safe & Caring Schools® Series
Activities for Building Character and Social-Emotional Learning
by Katia S. Petersen, Ph.D.

Build attitudes of respect and caring, reduce problem behaviors, empower students to solve problems, and educate the whole child socially, emotionally, and academically with these flexible, classroom-tested activity guides.

Each book: *S/C, 8½" x 11". Educators, group leaders, and caregivers, grades PreK–8. CD-ROM included.*

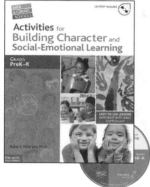
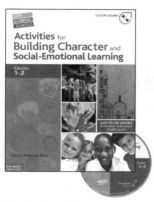
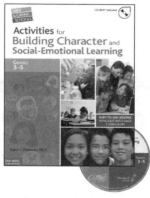
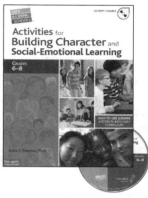

Grades PreK–K, 160 pp.   Grades 1–2, 208 pp.   Grades 3–5, 208 pp.   Grades 6–8, 208 pp.

The Safe & Caring Schools® Posters

Four posters reinforce the lessons and key skills from the Safe & Caring Schools resource guides. Use in classrooms, hallways, and gathering areas throughout the school. All posters are high gloss.

High gloss, 13⅜" x 19", Set of 4

Interested in purchasing multiple quantities?
Contact edsales@freespirit.com or call 1.800.735.7323 and ask for Education Sales.

Many Free Spirit authors are available for speaking engagements, workshops, and keynotes.
Contact speakers@freespirit.com or call 1.800.735.7323.

For pricing information, to place an order, or to request a free catalog, contact:

Free Spirit Publishing Inc. • 217 Fifth Avenue North • Suite 200 • Minneapolis, MN 55401-1299
toll-free 800.735.7323 • local 612.338.2068 • fax 612.337.5050 • help4kids@freespirit.com • www.freespirit.com

SKILLS FOR SCHOOL. SKILLS FOR LIFE.

PROFESSIONAL DEVELOPMENT

Staff Development and Consultation is available with author, Dr. Katia Petersen.

SCS workshops give schools and districts the tools, focus, and planning they need to implement an effective social and emotional learning approach. The options include the following:

LEADERSHIP OVERVIEW WORKSHOP

For administrators and district leaders who are interested in the benefits of integrating social, emotional, and academic learning and how the SCS program can help accomplish their school improvement goals. Participants will have the opportunity to create specific steps and action plans to help them build collaboration and communication among administrators, staff, parents, and students to support an ongoing process in creating systemic change.

SCS ON-SITE WORKSHOP

Implement a comprehensive social, emotional, and academic learning approach using the SCS program. Staff will learn practical and effective ways to create systemic change through infusion of social emotional learning into daily academic instruction.

TEACHER COACHING

Reduce stress and increase creativity among teachers. Hold a staff renewal workshop to bring the power of connection and collective wisdom back into teamwork and productivity back into the classroom.

TRAIN THE TRAINERS WORKSHOP

For educators, student support service professionals, and after-school programming staff, the workshop includes these topics:

- Teaching the SCS program effectively
- Philosophy and mission of Safe & Caring Schools
- Infusing social and emotional learning into academic subject areas
- Schoolwide and district-wide implementation steps
- Program sustainability

PARENT ENGAGEMENT

Reinforce a positive relationship between home and school by introducing parents and caregivers to the SCS approach. Help families practice and reinforce SCS skills at home.

For more information, visit www.safeandcaringschools.com or send an email to info@safeandcaringschools.com.